Bechanan
Camb., Mass.

D1180088

Human Dilemmas of Leadership

Human Dilemmas

of Leadership

by *Abraham Zaleznik*

Professor of Organizational Behavior
Harvard University Graduate School of
Business Administration

Affiliate Member and Research Fellow
Boston Psychoanalytic Society
and Institute, Inc.

HARPER & ROW, PUBLISHERS, NEW YORK AND LONDON

To

Bibs, Dori, and Ira

HUMAN DILEMMAS OF LEADERSHIP. *Copyright © 1966 by Abraham Zaleznik. Printed in the United States of America. All rights reserved. No part of this book may be used or reproduced in any manner whatsoever without written permission except in the case of brief quotations embodied in critical articles and reviews. For information address Harper & Row, Publishers, Incorporated, 49 East 33rd Street, New York, N.Y. 10016*

FIRST EDITION

LIBRARY OF CONGRESS CATALOG CARD NUMBER: 66-11480

C-Q

CONTENTS

Foreword

by
George P. Baker
Dean, Harvard Graduate School of Business Administration

This book presents a psychological study of leadership and the special problems facing individuals who are called upon to exercise authority in organizations. In introducing this volume to readers, there are several facts about the author that are of special interest.

Professor Zaleznik, who has been a member of the Faculty of the Harvard Graduate School of Business Administration for 19 years, has specialized in the study of human behavior in organizations. His research, writing, and teaching in this field have centered on the way individuals meet the opportunities and constraints posed by complex organizations. He has placed increasing emphasis on what the individual can do to fashion a more effective work and personal life. He does not see the individual as a passive object of the impersonal forces of big organizations, but is interested in the study of human and personal organizations as made up of active and responsible individuals who have a potential for controlling their destiny.

The point of view he presents in this book, while allied with humanistic and ethical principles, is based upon psychological contributions of a scientific nature. The particular psychology he applies is rooted in the clinical and theoretical concepts of psychoanalysis as developed by Sigmund Freud and his students.

In applying psychoanalysis to the study of human behavior in organizations, Professor Zaleznik is working on the frontiers of his field in two ways. First, he is attempting to develop a theory of organizations, with relevant applications to management, based upon the individual as the central unit of analysis. The chapters in this book deal with important organizational questions involving, for example, problems of power, authority, and dependency; tensions in group relationships; and analysis of leadership styles. But the analysis of these organizational problems uses the dynamic forces and developmental trends within the individual as the frame of reference.

The second way in which this work stands at the frontiers of his field is in the very fact that Professor Zaleznik's particular approach takes place in studies and teaching at a graduate school of business whose main concern is training managers and developing the knowledge to support a newly emerging profession.

Business management is obviously more than applied economics. In this same vein, it is also more than applied social science, if the disciplines related to the study of organizations ignore the complexity of human motivations and emotions in the collective efforts of men to control their environment. Work in the broad area of human behavior in organizations was started at the School as early as 1925 and has led to further avenues of research in many directions. So far as I know, the Harvard Business School is unique among the graduate business schools in having this pioneering work in applied psychoanalysis among the avenues of research which it has been prosecuting.

Professor Zaleznik's work has received continuing encouragement from the Harvard Business School. My immediate predecessor, Stanley F. Teele, lent support to the author when he began a candidacy at the Boston Psychoanalytic Society and Institute in 1960. As a result of his research work, Professor Zaleznik felt that his contribution to the study of organizations would be enhanced through formal training in psychoanalysis. He completed the program for non-medical candidates and with my encouragement continues at the Boston Psychoanalytic Society and Institute as a Research Fellow. In this capacity he is extending his research on work, career, and organizations in his training under supervision as a clinical psychoanalyst.

Many of the chapters in this book grow out of Professor Zaleznik's studies done under the auspices of the Division of Research of the Harvard Business School. He identifies, in his acknowledgment, publications of the Division of Research in which he presents in detail the concepts, methods, and findings of his research.

In writing this book, the author has tried to bridge the gap between technical research and the needs of professional managers. His audience is the person concerned with human problems in all kinds of organizations, including the professional manager in business. The method of presentation is designed to make otherwise highly technical material both readable and useful to busy executives.

I take a great deal of pleasure in introducing this volume and look forward to Professor Zaleznik's continuing work in this important area of study.

Soldiers Field, Boston

Acknowledgments

It is a pleasure to recognize the many generous people who have helped me in the preparation of this book. The administrative authorities of the Harvard Graduate School of Business Administration over the years have encouraged me to pursue my interests in the study of organizations. I am especially grateful to our former dean, Stanley F. Teele, and to our present dean, George P. Baker, whose foreword introduces this book to the reader. Professor Bertrand Fox, director of research, has also been of great help over the years in making it possible for me to carry on a substantial research program at the Harvard Business School. I have noted in text and footnotes throughout this book my work published by the division and its use as source material for the various chapters. There is no question that my motivation in writing this book related, in part at least, to a desire to integrate the separate research publications and to restate their findings for the general reader.

Two chapters (3 and 4) appeared originally as articles in the *Harvard Business Review*, and I appreciate Professor Edward P. Bursk's willingness on behalf of the editors of the *Review* to give me permission to revise and use these articles in this book. In a similar vein, the editors of *Behavorial Science* have granted me the rights to include as Chapter 9 a revised version of an article of mine that appeared in that journal in April 1964. I am grateful for this courtesy.

Dr. James Bushong and Dr. William Force, who are president and vice president respectively of the Kamehameha School in Honolulu, Hawaii, provided marvelous hospitality and good company while I taught in the Advanced Management Program of the University of Hawaii during the summers of 1964 and 1965. During my stay at Kamehameha I managed to write and revise several chapters in this book, and in thanking the people at Kamehameha, I want to remember especially Vicki Bushong and Rose Force, who were so kind to me and my family.

I owe a debt to Florence Glynn, who competently and cheerfully typed the final manuscript, as well as to Ann Allen, who helped in typing rough drafts of individual chapters. Ann Beale, who so fully appreciates the problems of a writer because she practices this craft herself, also typed chapters, prepared the index, and looked after the last-minute problems that arise when the editors, printers, and author worry about the publication deadline. In this connection, I am grateful to Richard McAdoo and his staff at Harper & Row for their willingness in undertaking the publication of this book.

I am, finally, grateful beyond words to a lot of people who variously have taught me, listened to me, and professed to have learned something from me in the course of my work as a student and teacher of human behavior.

With these expressions of gratitude go my best-felt affirmation of personal responsibility for the ideas in this book and their presentation.

ABRAHAM ZALEZNIK

Soldiers Field
Boston, Massachusetts
December 1965

. . . The evil that is in the world always comes of ignorance, and good intentions may do as much harm as malevolence, if they lack understanding. On the whole, men are more good than bad; that, however, isn't the real point. But they are more or less ignorant, and it is this that we call vice or virtue; the most incorrigible vice being that of an ignorance that fancies it knows everything and therefore claims for itself the right to kill. The soul of the murderer is blind; and there can be no true goodness nor true love without the utmost clear-sightedness.

—ALBERT CAMUS, in *The Plague*

Human Dilemmas of Leadership

1 / *Introduction*

The most self-conscious people in the world are its leaders. They may also be the most anxious and insecure. As men of action, leaders face risks and uncertainty, and often display remarkable courage in shouldering grave responsibility. But beneath their fortitude, there often lies an agonizing sense of doubt and a need to justify themselves.

Executives in business allude to these concerns when they refer to their life in the "goldfish bowl" as though they were constantly exposed to the scrutiny of others. Of course, those who depend upon leaders keep a close watch on their behavior, trying to read intent and meaning into words and actions. But this scrutiny from without may be quite trivial compared with the weight of self-observation.

The crux of leadership is the acceptance of responsibility—the idea or fantasy that one can make a difference in the course of events. This sense of personal involvement in life is not simply a passive experience. It is an impelling urge to make a difference and use oneself in effecting outcomes. The insecurity of leaders is often related to the possibility that their actions in the end may appear trivial.

What generally sustains leaders, besides their compulsive drive to get things done, is their quality of egoism. They have a more than usual degree of interest and fascination with their own motivations, character, and personality. This at times appears overbearing and selfish to others, yet it never fails to elicit an uncanny attraction most of us feel in the presence of "great men."

Egoism, or a heightened sense of self, is a dangerous game. When it appears graceful or powerful, it elicits strong emotions that bind the follower to the leader and gives over to him considerable influence. When it is awkward or meaningless, the egoism of the leader provokes ridicule and the urge to shame a pretender. The line between grace and power on the one hand, and awkwardness on the other, is faint, and leaders are usually aware of the tenuous quality of their egoism.

The danger in egoism is also related to the possibility that it may go beyond the limits of self-control and separate the individual from reality. The mad king is a fascinating figure in literature because all of us in the deeper reaches of awareness know something about the route traveled by powerful figures who have lost contact with reality.

The sense of responsibility, no matter how it is strengthened by personal confidence, is not easy to endure. Yet we find individuals in many occupations and walks of life who seem to master the resistances and anxieties associated with responsibility. Observation of these apparent instances of mastery heightens the desire to understand the experiences that lead to such expressions of individuality.

This book is about the tensions and conflict experienced in grasping for and acting upon the sense of responsibility. More broadly, it deals with the problems of achieving individuality in work, whether or not the person is formally an executive in an organization. Leadership is not restricted to the occupants of formal positions. It is mainly the process of influence—the capacity of men to alter the thoughts and actions of one another in the direction of some useful work. In this sense, the artist, the scientist, and other men of ideas rate consideration as leaders as well as executives and political figures.

The theme that unites such diverse figures of influence is the way each achieves a sense of his own uniqueness and learns to channel his individuality into creative work, like building an enterprise, asserting ideas, or organizing a nation.

The material in this book comes mainly from observation of leaders in business and industry. This is the center which has drawn most of my attention and with which I am most familiar. It is an especially appropriate source of material on leadership since these organizations are complex and demand the best possible performance from their executives.

Business organizations also serve as the stage upon which the conflicts of individuality are played out for many people. On the one hand, there seems to be a demand for conformity and identification with organizations that threatens the very essence of individuality—the sense of one's personal impact on events. On the other hand, organizations provide ample room for individuals to assert themselves and express their unique style of performance. The point is that organizations do not provide individuality as a gift. It has to be gained and even fought for while sustaining one's involvement and responsibility.

Curiously enough, organizations still depend for their vitality upon the small number of persons who actually succeed in developing a personal and individualistic approach to their work and life. Much is made today of the way organizations can be established to bring the best out of men. I prefer to turn the coin over and examine how great men, by the strength of their character and personality, remake organizations. In this sense, human personality may still be more powerful in fusing resources and opportunities leading to change then conceptions of the "healthy" or "creative" organizations.

The energy and vitality that make organizations move depend upon individual initiative. Leaders with brilliant ideas and the capacity to inspire thought and action in others are the main generators of energy. The effects of their personality induce a contagion to perform that is considerably stronger in directing organizations than depersonalized systems such as interlocking committee structures or participative management. The release of individual energy and the contagion to perform occur within organization structures. But the impulse and inspiration derive from individual personality.

In short, this book on leadership and individuality will adopt the vantage point of the person and his experience—an internal view of man as compared with an external view. It will emphasize the experience and conflicts of individual development in the setting of work and organizations. The main concern will be how the individual learns to get the feel of himself as a person and then proceeds to build outwardly rather than looking for cues and affirmations from his environment to govern his style of performance.

Not all individuals, in fact relatively few, secure a balance in favor of activity, self-assertion, and responsibility. But I intend neither to eulogize nor to judge. The basic problem is one of explanation—to know and understand the dilemmas of leadership and influence in human organizations. How this knowledge is used is up to the individual to decide.

2 / Conflicts in Work, Authority, and Self-Esteem

Generally speaking, there are two broad philosophies competing for acceptance as guides to the problems of man in organizations. These are the utopian and the individualistic views.

THE UTOPIAN VIEW

The utopian view asserts that man is inherently good and that the natural course of human life is toward personal growth or self-actualization. It is an optimistic assumption, because utopianism holds out for a kind of optimal position for man in which his natural tendencies yield increasingly high levels of productivity and creativity.

The basic problem of man in organization, according to those who hold the utopian view, derives squarely from certain properties of business organizations that act to constrain or block the individual. Business organizations create a culture opposed to the natural development of man toward this position of goodness, maturity, and creativity. This view further holds that understanding of the way in which organizations create constraints opposed to the natural tendencies of man will lead to the search for new models of organization more in harmony with man's basic tendency toward growth.

The constraints built into formal organizations are of two general types: structural conditions and value orientations. Structural conditions consist of the physical and social organization of work that govern the activities and relationships of men. Studies of mass production work, for example, seem to show that under a high degree of mechanization and job repetitiveness, individuals tend to develop major symptoms of social and personal pathology, such as absenteeism, turnover, complaints, illnesses, and accidents. Mechanization, it is argued, leaves little room for work expressivity for the individual, and limits his discretion. As a result, employees become apathetic and fail to achieve the autonomy characteristic of the mature adult.

The concern with technology as a block to individual development poses a dilemma; what appears constraining to the individual proves beneficial for the society. It is easily demonstrated that mechanization and mass production methodology form the very foundation of our industrial society. Without them, we could not have achieved the high levels of productivity necessary for our current standard of living. There are a few isolated instances of experimentation with new methods of production to overcome the negative effects, but these by and large have not proved very promising. Job enlargement is one such instance designed to reverse the effects of job repetitiveness.

Those who argue from the utopian view and who are concerned about structural factors also view with some alarm the increasing tendency toward automation as a continuation of this trend. For example, in clerical operations, the introduction of computers is changing the character of white-collar work. First of all, mechanization reduces the number of people formerly required to do a job, and second, those who remain are closely tied to a system with uncertain effects on the man-machine adjustment. I recently heard of a case involving a group of workers in a large office; these were relatively high-status people who were introducing a computer operation. Of fourteen workers, nine reported sick, and there were independent diagnoses presented of anxiety neuroses. This would be cited as a case of technology affecting adversely the individual's state of health.

Another type of structural constraint is the organization design in its effects on work and the individual. The argument advanced is that large-scale organizations are generally shaped in the form of pyramids, with power centered at the top. This centralization of power means that the control of activity and communication is held at the higher levels of organization and that, as one proceeds down the hierarchy, he finds the individual increasingly passive. The utopians view centralization of power, therefore, as a condition harmful to the individual on the grounds that the natural growth pattern in life is from passivity to activity.

Several remedies are offered as alternatives. Experiments with decentralization intend to redistribute power and control with less at the top and more at the lower levels of the organization. The main difficulty with experiments in decentralization is the new dilemma created for the leaders of industrial and business enterprises who feel responsible for the results of work and are under pressure to retain discretion for many kinds of decisions. It appears difficult, in other words, to lay out a flat and irrevocable pattern for delegating responsibility. I have considerable sympathy for executives in this dilemma because organizations are not inherently democratic. This situation places executives in the position of fostering experiments toward decentralization on the one hand, and acting in ways that appear superficially inconsistent with the experiments, on the other. As a result, we are confronted with the problem of executive mental health—the inner conflicts of individuals in doubt.

A large insurance company, in collaboration with a group of university-based social scientists, began a program of decentralization to include all levels of the organization. The intent was to bring clerical workers into the decision process following a plan of driving the responsibility for decisions as close to the point of implementation as possible. The management and the social scientists discovered, however, that employees began to interpret the experiment to mean that the individual had complete freedom in governing the conduct of his work. When employees finished their work, they would leave the job without regard for conventions of time and place. The experiment was abandoned abruptly with some bad feeling between the university people and the management.

The main problem with experiments in the distribution of power and authority is in the tendency to adopt an "all-or-nothing" attitude. This attitude reflects a basic antagonism to authority and effectively sabotages the innovations. As we know, every individual exists in a kind of uncertain position—he has some autonomy under certain conditions, but he is never free of commitments.

The concern with the structure of power and authority relations borders on the issue of values, the second main type of constraint under discussion among utopians. Value systems and beliefs held implicitly by authority figures prove more crucial to the outcome than the actual design of formal organization. If managers *assume* that employees are indolent, lazy, and incapable of growth, they will act according to these assumptions. This behavior, which includes one-way communication, overdirectiveness, and close supervision, stimulates behavior that confirms the initial assumptions. On the other hand, assumptions akin to the utopian philosophy will have the opposite effect and foster maturity and productivity.

This argument about the effects of values on the climate of human relationships has a certain charm and inherent optimism, because to alter values means a new atmosphere for work. The job then becomes one of education, persuasion, and indoctrination into the new set of values. Notice, however, that the object of change, the target for education is the manager, or the authority figure in organizations. Indirectly, at least, he is faced with a burden of guilt that is not conducive to education and learning.

It is not surprising that the individuals who find the value argument most attractive are those who identify with the subordinate in organizations and against the authority figure. I have found the late adolescent, because of his position in the life cycle, most enchanted by the attempts at reforming the authority figures of the world, and consequently enthusiastic supporters of this position. Similarly, I suspect many adults who support this value argument are themselves bound into real yet unresolved conflicts with authority. The urge for a new ideology displaces the problem of authority from oneself onto a somewhat malevolent object. While this displacement may produce some psychological comfort, it scarcely helps in understanding the nature of authority dilemmas (see Chapter 3).

Another difficulty with the utopian theme of value effects is the *a-historical* quality to the argument. It would seem as though individuals put on and shed beliefs and ideals as readily as clothing. The problem is not so simple because the tensions are indeed a product of history—the history of the person.

The Individualistic View

The alternate view of the problem of men in organizations may be called individualistic; the term may not be entirely appropriate, but it serves to highlight the contrast.

The individualistic view assumes that man is inherently neither good nor bad but is capable of assuming responsibility. It places the stress on individual action, choice, and freedom as the main center of concern in understanding man's relation to organizations. This point of view, I believe, is consistent with the basic psychology of Sigmund Freud, who developed, through clinical study and theory, a new understanding of man.

According to this psychology, motivation and behavior are products of the individual's history. Human development proceeds through the mastery of life tasks arising from biological as well as social processes. The way each successive life task is mastered provides the capacity for meeting and resolving new crises in development. The unresolved conflicts connected with mastery of the life tasks continue to intrude on further development even through the adult years of career and family responsibility.

Following this orientation, individual behavior is reasonable and understandable if one perceives in it the attempt to deal with certain continuities in personal history. A piece of behavior that looks irrational or puzzling to any of us, could be understood if we were able to jump inside the skin of the individual, so to speak, and grasp the meaning of his behavior in the light of his total history and total development.

Given the idea that man is a product of history does not mean that he behaves reflexively or that he has no choice and control over his destiny. Quite the contrary, he can master history and learn to use himself in ways quite consistent with the direction he seeks actively to go. Notice this point: The person can master history, and he can use history, but he is never *free* of history. He is constantly dealing with trends and experiences that he has to synthesize in some way or other.

The individualistic view focuses attention on the person in the man-organization interaction. This interaction goes in two directions. The individual is not only reacting to forces in his environment, but he is also acting on his environment in both positive and negative ways, and this two-way traffic is a crucial point in the argument. The individual not only *reacts* to his environment but he also *acts on* his environment. He acts positively in the sense of using the environmental opportunities to express himself and to achieve gratifications; he acts in a negative sense in that he can use his history and environment to express or perpetuate certain kinds of conflictual behavior. Perhaps an illustration will clarify this last idea.

Not too long ago, I was a consultant to a small company in which the management requested help in a program for improving the quality of the first-level supervision. As all of us are inclined to be skeptical of another man's diagnosis, especially of his own ailment, I agreed to undertake a preliminary study to determine the types of problems affecting supervisors.

I talked with most of the supervisors and it soon became evident that more serious problems detracting from company performance existed in the relationships among the top management. The executives, much as parents in some families, used their subordinates to display and perpetuate problems such as divided responsibility, hidden rivalry, and wasteful competition. We agreed to work directly on these problems before undertaking supervisory development work.

In the course of my meetings and interviews with supervisors, many important problems were clarified. One supervisor exemplified the individual who uses his environment in a negative way. In the course of talking about his job and his supervisory responsibilities, it became evident that he was upset about his status in the company. He made it clear that he felt he had been exploited in this organization. He described how he had been promised many rewards but that none of these promises had ever been kept. For instance, he had been promised a more responsible job and pay increases, but as yet he had no indication of specific future advancement. I did not comment much as he talked, since it is difficult to offer a sensible comment in response to real and intense feeling. Instead, I listened more carefully, and this supervisor began to describe other work experiences before joining this particular company. He had once worked for another company in which this pattern of exploitation also existed, and he then cited other instances in which he found himself exploited by a boss who appeared at one time as a kindly father-figure.

In this constant repetition of a theme in which the individual feels somewhat helpless and hopeless, as though he is a passive victim of experience ("things are always happening to me and I never know why . . ."), we have an instance, I believe, of the person unconsciously using his environment to play out, in a self-defeating way, an unresolved problem from his past. What such individuals are unable to recognize is the fact that their helplessness is a façade. The feeling of being victimized occurs only with their silent assent and manipulation. There seems to be an almost fateful desire to keep themselves enmeshed in a set of feelings that serves to mask their own responsibility in the situation. For substantial change to occur in his life situation would require the individual to achieve insight into his part in the problem.

In the individualistic view, the fateful encounter between man and organization turns on the capacity of the person to maintain and build upon a strong sense of self-esteem. The evaluations he makes of himself are tied closely to his ability to assume responsibility for his own development. But the aim of his activity is to secure reasonably consistent measures of influence over his environment.

We are not dealing with the developing individual in a vacuum, nor are we to assume that, because emphasis is placed on self-esteem, the environment can be ignored.

Two particularly relevant conditions in the organization are the changing content of work and the structure of authority relations. Organizations are purposive and directed toward achieving goals. The goals of the organization involve technologies and the application of crafts and skills that seem to have greater continuity than the contributions of particular individuals. Yet it is to the particular technology that the individual ties his efforts and seeks to implement his talents. As the nature of work changes, the individual is faced with new questions of adaptation, but work in fact changes only because of individuals who exercise their competence.

The individual entering an organization occupies a position in a social space. The definition of this space hinges largely on the dimension of authority—the boss, subordinates, and peers with whom he expects to transact business. The question of self-esteem seems continually to bump into the conceptions and acts of others.

The Changing Conditions of Work

The basic model of work by which the individual is trained in the course of his history is a simple one. It is a three-step model. First, there is tension activated within the individual; that is, the individual's needs within himself provoke or create tension. Second, this tension leads to action; he does something generally directed toward need satisfaction. Third, the action or the results of action lead to discharge of tension as a result of gratifications. These three steps form a basic model that characterizes work of any kind. The model appears in children's play, and as we know, play is the precursor of work. If one examines the play of children, the same three-step relationship appears. There is the tension or the need, activity, and discharge.

Work in modern organizations evolves under an extremely complex set of conditions. The complexities, of which I can identify six, increase the significance of the continuing psychological task facing the individual in maintaining the rhythm of this three-step model. The complexities are: first, the problem of time lag; second, the difficulties created by the indirect quality of feedback to the individual; third, the diffusion of control regulating work outcomes; fourth, the quality of interdependence surrounding work activity; fifth, the problem of technical obsolescence; and finally, the related sixth problem of role obsolescence.

Time Lag

The nature of work in organizations makes it necessary for the individual to sustain tension for longer periods of time as compared with the requirements of the more simplified forms of industrial organization. This tension results from the time lag between activity and outcomes. This time lag is a feature of work involving ideas rather than material things.

Transactions with ideas, which were once restricted to creative workers in the arts and sciences, now characterize the job of executives. Most of the time, managers deal with symbols and concepts in formulating strategies, communicating thoughts, and arriving at decisions. Instead of discharging tensions, activity tends to increase the intensity of motivations that must be sustained in the face of uncertainty about the wisdom of executive plans and decisions.

The generation of tension and its reverberations throughout an organization are important stress factors. The executives least likely to be able to bear this stress are, paradoxically, those who seem most needful. This quality of needfulness appears to other as impatience, greed, and hyperactivity. The impatience and greediness are sometimes manifested in overeating, excessive drinking and smoking, as though the oral intake eases the hunger for closure in the evaluation of one's work efforts.

Indirect Feedback

Closely akin to the stress caused by the time lag between activity and outcomes is the ambiguous and indirect quality of the feedback one receives. The individual may see few direct results of his activity, especially where clear-cut responsibility for work is not easily established. There are all sorts of forces over which executives have little control. Many times these forces can act in favor of them or against them.

For example, in a medium-sized company with a successful history, the president conducted a careful and deliberate cycle of planning a new stock issue. The proposed stock sale was tied to the transition from a family enterprise to a public corporation with important consequences for planning as well as corporate growth. The president and advisers deliberated at length on issuing stock and just when plans were about to be realized, there was a sudden collapse in the market, which resulted in the suspension of the sale.

Such circumstances are not unusual and suggest the kind of balance and maturity needed to sustain the stress produced by forces over which the individual has little control.

Diffusion of Control

The presence in modern organizations of diverse interest groups accounts for still another source of stress on the individual. Organizatons cannot be considered democratic institutions and have no clearly defined constitutional basis. Yet, the processes of organizations set up an implicit system of checks and balances through the influence exerted by interest groups.

The system of checks and balances through which work moves is centered in the diverse populations of the corporation. Each population acts as a reference group and provides much of the content for the consolidation of the individual's identity. In one corporation that had rapidly changed from a consumer product and marketing organization to a vertically integrated industrial complex, the employees identified themselves with a series of subgroups contending for supremacy. There were the old-timers who were the shrewd, intuitive marketers, supported by a traditional production subgroup. A group of newcomers consisted of professional engineers, scientists, and managers. College-trained, including a liberal sprinkling of Ph.D.'s, this subgroup of newcomers thought, worked, and reacted in entirely different ways than the old-timers. Any single individual acting in his capacity as an executive found himself bound into the implicit struggle for control. As in so many similar situations, the old-timers appeared to maintain control through exertion of pressures that made work in this company unpleasant for the new group. As a result, the turnover rate among professionals was high and discouraged the consolidation of the new breed in this company.

The pressures exerted by interest groups on corporate activity extend beyond the boundaries of the organization to include government, customers, and the public. Corporate executives, for example, cannot ignore the effects of the civil rights movement in decisions on plant location. The scientist and engineer in industry may sense only vaguely the relationship between discussions in a congressional committee on the space program and the fate of a contract in his work group. He experiences this connection concretely, however, if the government contract is canceled and his work group no longer has a reason for existence and is disbanded.

For the individual, success or failure may appear less related to competence and effort and more to forces over which he has seemingly little control. Such a situaton of diffusion of control can lead to feelings of discouragement unless the person has the sort of perspective that we ordinarily associate with an educated mind.

Interdependence

Many observers of industry view the diffusion of control as a fact of life and are prepared to examine its implications for the individual and organizations. Others, however, applaud this subtle shift in the work structure as an example of man's increasing interdependence. I would be more cautious in calling this change a good thing.

Interdependence is a stressful factor for certain individuals. The idea men in organizations, frequently very creative individuals, concentrate their emotional investments in the work itself in constrast to the human relationships surrounding work. Dealing with other persons is taxing for them and not a major source of satisfaction. For other individuals, work apart from human contact means nothing and in fact is painful.

It is all too easy to decide that this latter type of person, who often seeks administrative work, is the standard for judging all others. But without the idea men, who basically derive pleasure from work alone or with few like-minded individuals, we would soon discover a general decay in the effectiveness of organizations.

Technical Obsolescence

A fifth source of stress on the individual grows out of the chronic problem of technical obsolescence. There is today an uncertainty about the usefulness of the individual's skills and competence over a lifetime of work.

The classic form of technical obsolescence hits the blue-collar worker following the introduction of technological change. But the more highly-educated employees are now also subject to technical obsolescence. The professional engineer or scientist who graduates from a major institute may find after five or ten years that new knowledge and techniques in his field have outdated his training.

More recently, the prospects of technical obsolescence have affected management. With new methods of data processing and decision making there may be underway a new trend toward centralization. This brings into question the character of the middle management job for the future, and raises doubts about the effectiveness of managers who are unfamiliar with these newer decision approaches.

Role Obsolescence

Technical obsolescence as a stressful event for the individual is a visible problem and the subject of much public discussion. A more subtle form of obsolescence, one less noticeable yet severe in its impact is role obsolescence. The term "role" is used here to denote the organized patterns of behavior of an individual who occupies a position in a social structure. The position, defined variously in terms of occupation, family, and community, carries with it a set of expectations concerning the duties and privileges associated with the position. A role becomes obsolete when conditions in the social structure bypass or devalue the activities formerly connected with the position, and in this sense is similar to the effects of technological change on the individual. Role obsolescence occurs also when other persons are no longer able or willing to respond to the individual in a reciprocal fashion with some mutuality of interest. A father, for example, cannot perform the work of fatherhood without the reciprocity of a son who can respond in the forms that enhance the relationship between father and son.

Business organizations are constantly in flux in the structure and dynamics of role relationships. Contrary to many ideas in the literature, these organizations are highly personal and human situations to those who live and work in them. Individuals come and go, and experience changes in themselves as they get older. This movement and flow forces upon the person a continuing pressure to engage in a kind of internal "work," where self-appraisal and introspection become the means for altering a pattern of attitudes and behavior. It may seem strange to use the term "work" in this way, but role work consumes energy and in a vital form, sometimes to the point where the individual's existence depends on how well he carries out this silent performance. It is not at all uncommon to find that events leading to sudden role obsolescence, such as loss of a loved one, or being sidetracked in an organization produce enough stress to precipitate a breakdown.

In discussing the changing qualities of work in organizations as sources of stress upon the individual, I have suggested throughout the difficulty in maintaining a work rhythm based upon the simple three-step model of (1) activation of need and tension; (2) goal directed activity; (3) satisfaction of needs, and the discharge of tension. Complex work structures are an inherent quality of large-scale organizations, and the issue of stress management is one of the challenges of maturation to the individual. Of equal significance are the implications of authority relationships in organizations, a subject to which I shall turn at this point in the chapter.

AUTHORITY RELATIONS IN LARGE ORGANIZATIONS

Work within an organizational hierarchy places a burden upon the individual to learn to manage differences in status and power. Every individual has a boss and in fact, he usually has more than one power figure to whom he feels responsible. Similarly, the person works intimately with subordinates whose activity he directs and for whom he takes responsibility in evaluation of their efforts. The individual is also connected in lateral transactions with persons who are similar in status.

I shall present in three separate chapters more detailed discussion of the psychological problems of authority, subordinacy, and equality. But in this chapter we need to outline broadly how authority relations act as sources of stress affecting the continuing struggle for a sense of individuality. The basic issues are the balance between independence and dependence, and the experience of rivalry.

Independence and Dependence

Within a hierarchy the individual must learn to strike a balance between the conflicting wishes for independence and dependence in relationships with authority figures. This conflict has its historical roots in the experience in the family. The initial encounter in the family involves a dependent position in relation to mother and father. Gradual transition to a more independent position includes establishing wider relationships outside the family and assuming greater degrees of responsibility, until the balance is securely in favor of adulthood.

But it would be a mistake to view the transition from dependency to independence as a "once and for all" piece of psychological work. The desires for a nurturant and passive relationship with others never disappear entirely. Failure to recognize and deal with the dependent-passive yearnings leads to their appearance in disguised forms. The frequency of the so-called "executive stomach ulcer" is a case in point. Studies of conflicts underlying the outbreak of ulcers show the presence of marked unconscious wishes for passive dependency.

Somewhat less disguised are the sudden outbreaks of depression in the adult male. Here, the individual seemed to have functioned quite effectively throughout his life but upon reaching his middle forties, a sense of disappointment overwhelms him and appears as a depression with loss of interest in work and human relationships.

It may appear paradoxical at first glance to suggest that dependency yearnings if unrecognized can lead to trouble, while if given into can lead to marked reductions in effectiveness as an adult, particularly in the ability to transform infantile wishes into those forms that are useful for the present life situation. Giving into the infantile dependency wishes leads to the characteristics of passivity, submissiveness to authority figures, inability to arrive at independent judgments, and anonymity. Reacting against these wishes leads to the eruption of conflict in physical and emotional disturbance, including excessive fatigue and work disabilities.

The effective use of dependency in the adult is reflected in his ability to learn from someone in authority who has, through experience and competence, something to teach. It is also reflected in the ability to relax, take vacations, and passive recreation. This use of dependency provides a fund of energy for the opportunities of active work, which include teaching subordinates as well as making decisions.

The basic defect that occurs in authority relations in organizations is the failure to achieve the balance in the drives for independence and dependence. The organization provides ample opportunity to work on this problem or to oscillate between two unsatisfactory extremes. Dependence as a modal character resolution in the adult is usually unsatisfactory, because it involves excessive leaning upon others and an inability to assume initiative. The dependency solution generally results in manipulations and counter-manipulations between superior and subordinate with gross distortions of important work processes.

Similarly extreme independence, characterized usually by overt rebellion against authority figures and hostility toward subordinates creates different problems with the high degree of interdependence in organizations. Unless conditions in the organization demand rebellion and change, the independent individual experiences authority relations as very stressful.

Rivalry

For dependent individuals visible responsibility is a source of stress. They do not particularly seek the initiative for activity and therefore find burdensome organizational demands of this kind.

For the highly independent individuals, the reverse condition is experienced as stress—the condition where control and responsibility are not in their hands. Under such circumstances struggles for power engender intense rivalrous feelings.

Some colleagues and I conducted a study in one organization that included questions about how individuals assess the distribution of power in their immediate relationships with superiors and subordinates. Superior-subordinate sets were defined by the actual organization chart. Each member of the set was asked to indicate how much power and authority he felt he had as compared with the other person in the set in making important organization decisions. The responses of the set were compared and resulted in the classification of three types of authority relations: (1) congruent; (2) abdicative; (3) competitive.

The congruent relationships consisted of agreement in the responses of both the superior and subordinate in the set on divisions of authority and responsibility. The chief feature of the congruent pattern was the absence of felt rivalry between superior and subordinate. Most of the congruent responses were identified with individuals who had achieved an orientation in their work careers. The other two types appeared frequently among individuals who were in the midst of career difficulties.

The "abdicative" response occurred when both superior and subordinate in a relationship attributed authority to the counterpart and assumed little for themselves. Abdication occurred frequently among the passive-dependent type of personality. While overt rivalry appeared absent, the incorporation of personal responsibility in relation to job functions also appeared absent.

The third type of authority relationship, called "competitive," did involve conditions of felt rivalry between superior and subordinate. The distinguishing feature of this type consisted of an assumption of authority on the part of each respondent in the set and little attribution of responsibility to the counterpart. The individuals in competitive authority relationships seemed involved in career conflicts with strong ambivalent attitudes toward authority on the surface. The competitors assumed an active-independent stance; unconsciously there appeared strong fears and concerns for their own masculine independence. Fears of being submissive toward authority figures were quite evident along with real doubts about their ability to sustain an aggressive position in work and family relationships. Here the contrast between conscious intentions and self-representations on the one hand, and unconscious fantasy on the other reveal the meaning of the rivalry.

An important feature of this typology of response to authority is its direct relevance to individual developmental conflicts. These conflicts can be understood as an aspect of individual experience and personal history. While expressing the conflicts in work relationships, their cause could not be attributed especially to particular constraints in organization structure. The problem of authority understood historically is a problem in large measure of individual development and less, as the utopians would assume, caused by the "here and now" constraints of organization life.

However a particular problem of authority is manifested, the pressure for its resolution rests squarely on the shoulders of the individual. In the final analysis he must account for the rewards and costs implied in any mode of resolution whether it be the extremes of dependence-passivity or independence-assertiveness, or some effective balance. It is of little value to propose a kind of general structural solution apart from capacities of individuals to use their enviroment wisely and maturely.

I will develop further in the next two chapters how authority problems become evident in organizations and their roots in developmental problems of the individual. I have tried to show in this chapter that the individualistic view of the dilemmas of man in organizations revolves around the process of building and maintaining self-esteem in the face of frequently stressful situations in the environment. The stress, however, is not to be confused with the causes and resolution of esteem problems. These are essentially the continuing tasks of individual development.

What are the major elements in the process of building and maintaining the sense of self-esteem? What consistent themes in development carry over into the individual's work life in modern organizations? Let us turn to a discussion of these questions as they are basic to an understanding of the individualistic view of work, authority and self-esteem.

THE PROBLEM OF SELF-ESTEEM

A continuing struggle to enhance the sense of self-esteem goes on between the individual and the organization. The main focus of the adult in his work and career is to establish awareness of himself as a unique individual while contributing to his society. The complete merger of his identity within any social structure results in a gradual loss of feeling and responsibility. This loss reverberates throughout the entire life performance of the individual at work, in the family, and the community.

An extreme example of identity through membership with the loss of individual responsibility is presented to us in the case of Adolph Eichmann. In the name of a bureaucracy and his position in it, he was capable of the most heinous crimes. Yet the crimes, horrible as they were, took second place in comparison to the absence of awareness and guilt over his actions.

Another view of this loss of responsibility and individuality in the fusion with an organization is afforded in the study of the compulsive personality. On the surface, the compulsive character is a compliant, pleasant, and obedient type of person who speaks in the metaphor of cooperation and good feeling. Beneath this veneer is a continuing devaluation of himself as a person. The attempts to conform and become something through a membership in an organization result from an underlying sense of nothingness at the core of his existence. He suffers from a paucity of conscious feelings and seeks to remain alive in belonging to a system. A closer study of such individuals reveals a hard core of anger and hostility. The compulsive individual cannot accept initiative and responsibility because the life pattern is drawn into avoidance of his own inner world.

The lack of self-esteem is a failure in development. It exists in the here and now of a person's relationship to his work, but the center of this problem resides in the historical development of the individual. Historically speaking, we have to go back to early family relationships to examine how the individual experienced and dealt with gratifications and disappointments, particularly in relationships with parents. The basic disappointments fateful in the evolution of self-esteem are in the separation from mother, of the sense of limited control over others, and of being relatively helpless in the world of adults. The disappointments may result in the strengthening of the individual through his capacity to wait and experience his own development as these are supported by identifications with strong parents. Or, the individual may emerge weakened by a lingering sense of having left behind some desirable state of grace whose attraction is sometimes greater than the hard-won rewards of reality.

The gratifications and disappointments of development can be described another way, in terms of four polarities of human existence: (1) of giving and getting; (2) of controlling and being controlled; (3) of competing and cooperating; (4) of producing and facilitating. These polarities define the psychological space within which the work of securing individuality proceeds. These polarities are significant in the work life of the adult and warrant attention.

The Polarity of Giving and Getting

The mature individual in the organized settings of work and career enhances the sense of self-esteem through achieving a balance between giving and getting. The idea of giving or providing rewards for others without the sense of also getting impoverishes the person.

This impoverishment is seen most clearly in the false altruism of individuals who appear dedicated solely to the gratification of others. The altruism is false because it is based on repressing one's own legitimate wishes and consequently starving the ego. This type of altruism covers up a massive feeling of worthlessness and guilt that is tolerated through systematic self-deprivation.

The opposite type of imbalance, the extreme of getting without giving reflects the kind of needful personality I referred to earlier in this discussion. Here it would seem as though the danger of impoverishing the personality would not exist, since the needful individual appears singularly determined to gain self-gratifications in the form of esteem from others, status, and the more tangible rewards of income and ownership. Yet, paradoxically, the impoverishment of personality exists because the need is insatiable in the exchange of adult rewards and gratifications. The individual takes but remains unsatisfied.

This edge of unfulfillment reflects impoverishment of personality in still another way. The drive for reward reflects an incapacity of the ego to control needs and to channel the underlying tension into useful forms of work. This incapacity to bind tension and utilize energy productively leads to impoverishment on at least two counts: (1) the failure to develop flexible approaches to work, well tuned to the individual's personal style and the realities of constructive effort; (2) the failure to achieve enduring rewards that result from the expression of competence. The individual therefore remains needful and impulsive, chained to the ever-present demands of the psyche.

The Polarity of Controlling and Being Controlled

The sense of self-esteem as it evolves in the face of complex stresses of work and organizations depends in part on the issue of control. The feeling of complete control over one's own destiny and events in work organizations is pure illusion.

This illusion of control and efforts to secure complete dominance over events accounts for much of the needless proliferation of bureaucratic systems and procedures in organizations.

The opposite extreme, the sense of being controlled, appears as the illness of modern bureaucracy. There is some truth to this characterization, especially since the over-controlling personality attempts to train others to yield autonomy. But individuals are not compelled into passivity. Giving in to external control, experienced in the extreme as depersonalization and feeling victimized, is a response of the individual in relation to his own development. It aptly describes the condition where the quest for individuality has been abandoned. The alternative, the mode of self-assertion, requires the capacity to assume a stance and to maintain it in the face of the conflicting opinions and opposition that typify work. To achieve the degree of control that harmonizes with reasonableness on the one hand, and the need for self-assertion on the other is essential to the sense of self-esteem; this balance in control is both an outcome and requirement of individuality.

The Polarity of Competing and Cooperating

Most organizations place strong emphasis on the value of co-operation. The individual is then called upon to subordinate his interests in the course of some higher goal of a group. Cooperation is fostered in the family to help individuals delay their own need satisfactions in favor of weaker members of the group or to sustain the rhythm of family life. The playground and the school join parents in stressing the importance of cooperation. So the individual is well versed in the rationale of group purpose and altruism by the time he enters the world of work.

What is often overlooked by those who foster these attitudes of cooperation is the difficulty for individuals to live exclusively by these attitudes. The demands of competition and self-assertion are also significant in the conduct of a successful career. It is true that competition is experienced during early developmental phases, but in ways that frequently are hitched to group rituals and controls. Individual competition and the underlying aggressive impulses tend to be muted and even repressed. The fact that the aggressive impulses are a prominent feature of development well before the more socialized attitudes of cooperation and altruism—attitudes borrowed from loved parents and sustained at the cost of loss of love—results frequently in rigid compliance.

The cost of this compliance may be individuality and productivity. Rigid cooperative behavior, in other words, exists as a necessity in maintaining the individual's personal organization. It no longer functions as a useful way of approaching many types of life situations.

Starting with early development and continuing throughout the mature years, the individual faces the continual task of achieving his own unique balance between conflicting attitudes and modes of behavior. The success of this psychological work enables the individual to sustain himself and to foster his uniqueness. At the same time, he enhances his contributions to family and organizations through personal productiveness and the use of himself as an example.

The Polarity of Producing and Facilitating

Another theme in building self-esteem, closely related to cooperation-competition, is the polarity of producing and facilitating. Many individuals tend to settle at one or the other of the extremes, each with its own peculiar rewards and costs. Producing work identifiable with one's own energy and competence provides enormous ego gratifications. However, productivity and hard work that grow out of a need to avoid more passive thought process, or human contact, generally exact a heavy toll in wasted energy. The hard work may go only into repetitive channels, avoiding new experiences and challenges. Or, it may serve as a barrier to awareness of self as a means of separating rather than integrating different levels of personality. The outcome tends to be one of stilted performance and awkwardness rather than style and grace. The compulsive worker, in other words, experiences his effort as a lonely dance with a shadowy piper, whose tune and rhythm become unpredictable.

Other perils and compulsions await individuals who seek to adapt to the demands of work and organizations at the other extreme of the dichotomy. This extreme appears altruistic in the sense that the individual organizes his life and rationalizes his existence as facilitating the work of others. The individual thinks of himself as a catalyst, or a coach. His product in life is in training of others.

To be sure, there are work roles in which the theme of facilitating predominates. Teaching is a good example of such a role. I am reminded frequently how important facilitating is to many who liken their profession to farming—they prepare the soil, sow the seed, and cultivate. The outcome—growth—is then a mysterious work and the producer remains anonymous. Many executives in business along with teachers see themselves mainly in terms of facilitating or helping others to produce.

What may not be too apparent in the human appeal of the role of facilitator is its existence as a necessity rather than as a gain of development. In my experience, the facilitator who rationalizes and protects his reason for being in extremely passive terms suffers a lingering sense of disappointment. There once were goals and aspirations, but these had to be abandoned because of anxiety. Somehow, the theme of personal productiveness became involved in a false psychological equation: "If I produce, it is at someone else's expense; if I am strong someone else becomes weak."

Conclusion

I have tried in this chapter to establish the individual as the arena in which the conflicts of work and authority relationships get fought out. The stress of work and the pressures of authority in organizations are real. Their reality is in the experiencing of stress and its conversion into fruitful psychological work. The individual incorporates relevant and conflicting aspects of his environment, fuses them with trends in his own development, to produce a synthesis uniquely his own. He is an individual who affects his environment, rather than a passive agent who responds to forces completely outside himself.

The point of view about man in organizations that stresses individual responsibility constantly challenges our notions of the causes of ills in society. This view refuses to accept utopian and easy solutions. More important, it accepts human tension and conflict as a condition of existence and as an opportunity for change and progress. The emphasis is on the individual learning to assume responsibility and learning to exercise choice. His aid in this endeavor is education, and I include in this category the quest for knowledge about man in general and himself in particular.

3 / *The Human Dilemmas of Leadership** *

A few years ago, the citizens of the United States and of the world were witnesses to a political drama that had all the ingredients of a first-class tragedy. Were it not for the fact that the episode revealed some sense of the nature of power conflicts among influential men, one could safely have stopped reflections on the event at the point where its human interest ended and its deeper significance for leadership began. I am referring to the Adlai Stevenson episode that exploded on the public scene with an article in the *Saturday Evening Post* by Stewart Alsop and Charles Bartlett.[1]

In the course of the Stevenson affair, we became privy to backstage rivalry among subordinates close to the President. We saw attempts at political homicide and character assassination through the use of "the leak" of so-called secret positions in the deliberations of high councils of government. We saw the President of the United States drop his guard, if only momentarily, to show us how difficult it is to make or hold friends while in the Presidency. And throughout the revelations, charges, and countercharges we learned just what the medium of exchange can be in power conflicts; namely, prestige, personal integrity, friend-

* Adapted from the article "The Human Dilemmas of Leadership" in the July–August 1963 issue of the *Harvard Business Review,* © 1963 by the President and Fellows of Harvard College, reprinted by permission.
[1] "In Time of Crisis," Dec. 8, 1962, p. 15.

ship and loyalty, jealousy and egotism—all typical human sentiments likely to be found in any human encounter where people care about what they are doing.

In the professional literature on the job of the executive, one seldom finds much reference to or intelligent discussion of the dilemmas posed by the exercise of power and authority. The dramatists, novelists, biographers, and journalists attempt to portray these struggles in their works, but much is left to the sensitivity and intuition of the audience. And least of all are we ever invited to consider the underlying dynamics of leadership dilemmas and the different forms open to us for their resolution.

I should like to try to lift the veil somewhat on the nature of conflicts in exercising leadership. The two points I want to develop are:

1. The main source of the dilemmas leaders face is found within themselves, in their own inner conflicts.

2. Dealing more intelligently with knotty decisions and the inevitable conflicts of interest existing among men in organizations presupposes that executives, at least the successful ones, are able to put their own houses in order. It presupposes that the executive is able to resolve or manage his inner conflicts so that his actions are strongly grounded in reality, so that he does not find himself constantly making and then undoing decisions to the service of his own mixed feelings and to the disservice and confusion of his subordinates.

TENDENCY TO PROJECT

Most of us are accustomed by virtue of our training and inclinations to externalize conflicts and dilemmas. If an executive finds himself immobilized in the face of a difficult problem, he is apt to look to the outside for an explanation. He might perhaps say to himself that he is unable to act because he has inadequate authority delegated to him. Or he might hesitate because he feels subordinates are holding out on him by providing too little information, confused positions, and mixed signals. In this case, he is likely to vent his frustrations on their incompetence.

This generalized tendency to place conflicts in the outside world is part and parcel of the well-known mechanism of *projection*. A person projects when, unknown to himself, he takes an attitude of his own and attributes it to someone else. In the example just cited, the executive who despairs because his subordinates are confused and who charges them with holding back and with indecision may well be reading his own state of mind and attributing it to others.

It is not within us to be able consistently to separate those issues which arise from our own concerns from those issues that occur in surrounding situations. Let me cite another example:

The president of a large company was concerned with the possibility that his organization had failed to develop executive talent. This concern of his arose in connection with his own retirement. He organized a committee composed of assistants to vice presidents to study this problem and to report to him with recommendations.

The president's forthcoming retirement was well known, and there was private speculation as to who among the vice presidents would be named as his successor. This succession obviously implied that several persons among the assistant vice presidents would be promoted. The task force met several times but its discussions were not too productive or interesting. The group spent most of its time attempting to define what the president wanted the committee to do, instead of dealing with the issues the organization faced in attracting and developing executive talent.

In other words, they projected their own concerns and anxiety onto the president and attributed to him confused motives in undertaking the assessment of the company's needs in executive development. In reality the individuals themselves shared confused motivations. They were in intensive rivalry with one another over who among their immediate superiors would become president and how this change would affect their fate in the organization.

By centering attention on the inner conflicts of the executive, I do not mean to imply that conflicts are not based in the relations among individuals at work. The illustrations presented so far clearly indicate how vicious these relations may become. The point is that external conflicts in the form of power struggles and rivalry are more easily understood and subject to rational control when the executive is able to separate the conditions within himself from those existing on the outside.

This process of separation is more easily said than done. Nevertheless it is crucial for the exercise of leadership, and sometimes the separation is the very condition for survival. One wonders, for example, whether the failure to maintain this separation lay at the basis of the breakdown and subsequent suicide of such a brilliant man as James Forrestal. At the very least, by attending to the conditions within himself, the executive can expect to be dealing with those situations most susceptible to his rational control. It is in the long run a lot easier to control and change oneself than it is to control and change the world in which we live.

Forms of Inner Conflict

Before we examine some of the ways in which a man can learn to deal more competently with his inner life, we need to know something more about the nature of inner conflicts. Let us take two types that are quite prevalent among executives in organizations: *status anxiety*, those dilemmas frequently experienced by individuals at or near the top in their organizational world; *competition anxiety*, the feelings generated while climbing to the top.

These two prevalent types of anxiety, while resembling each other in a number of respects, are worth keeping separate for purposes of furthering understanding.

STATUS ANXIETY

When an individual begins to achieve some success and recognition in his work, he may suddenly realize that a change has occurred within himself and in his relations with associates. From a position of being the bright young man who receives much encouragement and support he, almost overnight, finds himself viewed as a contender by those who formerly acted as mentors. A similar change takes place in his relations with persons who were his peers. They appear cautious with him, somewhat distant, and constrained in their approach, where once he may have enjoyed the easy give-and-take of their friendship. The individual in question is then ripe for status anxiety. He becomes torn between the responsibilities of a newly acquired authority and the strong need to be liked.

There is a well-established maxim in the study of human behavior that describes this situation tersely and even poetically: "Love flees authority." Where one individual has the capacity to control and affect the actions of another, either by virtue of differences in their positions, knowledge, or experience, then the feeling governing the relationhip tends to be one of distance, and perhaps respect, but not one ultimately of warmth and friendliness.

This basic dichotomy between respect or esteem and liking is not easily changed. The executive who confuses the two is bound to get into trouble. Yet in our culture today we see all too much evidence of people seeking to obscure the difference. Much of the current concept of success equates popularity and being liked with competence and achievement. In Arthur Miller's *Death of a Salesman*, Willy Loman in effect was speaking for our culture when he measured a person's achievement in the gradations of being liked, well liked, or very well liked.

Reaction and Recognition

In what ways do executives react when they are caught in the conflict between exercising authority and being liked?

Sometimes they seek to play down their authority and play up their likability by acting out the role of the "nice guy." This is sometimes called status stripping, where the individual tries in a variety of ways to discard all the symbols of his status and authority. This ranges from proclaiming the open-door policy, where everyone is free to visit the executive anytime he wants, to the more subtle and less ritualistic means such as democratizing work by proclaiming equality of knowledge, experience, and position. And yet these attempts at status stripping fail sooner or later. The executive may discover that his subordinates join in gleefully by stripping his status and authority to the point where he becomes immobilized, is prevented from making decisions, is faced with the prospect of every issue from the most trivial to the most significant being dealt with in the same serious vein. In short, problem solving and work become terrorized in the acting out of status stripping.

The executive soon becomes aware of another aspect of his dilemma. Much to his horror, he finds that attempts to remove social distance in the interests of likability have not only reduced work effectiveness, but that his subordinates gradually come to harbor deep and unspoken feelings of contempt toward him. He inadvertently has provided them with a negative picture of what rewards await them for achievement. In effect, the process of status stripping helps to destroy the incentives for achievement and in the extreme can produce feelings of helplessness and rage.

There is yet another side to the dilemma of status anxiety which is well worth examining. This side has to do with the hidden desire to "touch the peak." Executives frequently want to be near the source of power and to be accepted and understood by their bosses. Such motivations lead to excessive and inappropriate dependency bids. Under such conditions, communication between superior and subordinate tends to break down.

So far we have discussed the problem of status anxiety as an aspect of seeking friendship, warmth, and approval from subordinates and bosses. Status anxiety is also frequently generated by the fear of aggression and retaliation on the part of persons who hold positions of authority. Executives sometimes report feeling lonely and detached in their position. A closer look at the sense of loneliness reveals a feeling that one is a target for the aggression of others. This feeling occurs because the executive is called upon to take a position on a controversial issue and to support his stand. He must be able to take aggression with a reasonably detached view, or the anxiety can become intolerable.

If in your experience you have encountered an executive who seemed unable to take a stand on a problem, who seemed to equivocate or to talk out of two sides of his mouth at once, then the chances are reasonably good that you have come upon a man in the throes of status anxiety. Sometimes this will appear in the form of hyperactivity—the case of the executive who flits from problem to problem or from work project to work project without really seeing an activity through to completion. In this case, the executive is utilizing the tactic of providing a shifting target so that other persons have difficulty in taking aim at him.

Constructive Approach

To refer to aggression and the avoidance of aggression as aspects of status anxiety, does not imply hostile aggression. It suggests instead that all work involves the release of aggressive energy. Solving problems and reaching decisions demand a kind of give-and-take where positions are at stake and where it is impossible for everyone concerned to be equally right all the time. But having to give way or to alter a position in the face of compelling argument is no loss. The executive who can develop a position, believe in it, support it to its fullest, and then back down, is a strong person.

This type of person does not suffer from status anxiety. He may love to provide a target because he knows this may be an effective catalyst for first-class work accomplishment. He is secure enough to know that he has nothing to lose but much to gain in the verve and excitement of interesting work. This type of executive is able to take aggression, and in fact encourage it, because he probably has abandoned the magical thinking that seems to equate his position of authority with omnipotence. No one has the power to make everyone else conform to his wishes, so it is no loss to learn that one has been wrong in the face of the arguments aggressively put forth by others. In fact, such ability to retract a stand results in heightened respect from others.

In other words, we should not be misled into equating the virtue of humility with executive behavior that appears modest, uncertain of a stand, and acquiescent toward others—behavior which frequently is feigned modesty to avoid becoming a target. True humility is marked by the person who thinks his way through problems, is willing to be assertive, is realistic enough to encourage assertiveness from others, and is willing to acknowledge the superiority of ideas presented by others.

COMPETITION ANXIETY

The second main pattern of inner conflict that badly needs attention is competition anxiety, a close kin of status anxiety. Competition exists in the give-and-take of solving problems and making decisions. It also exists in the desire to advance into the more select and fewer positions at the top of a hierarchy. An executive who has difficulty in coming to terms with a competitive environment will be relatively ineffective.

From my observations of executives—and would-be executives —I have found two distinct patterns of competition anxiety: (1) the fear of failure; (2) the fear of success. Let us examine each in turn.

Fear of Failure

You have perhaps seen the fear of failure operate in the activities of the child, where this type of problem generally originates.

The child may seem to become quite passive and unwilling to undertake work in school or to engage in sports with children his age. No amount of prodding by parents or teachers seem to activate his interests; in fact, prodding seems to aggravate the situation and induce even greater reluctance to become engaged in an activity. When this child progresses in school, he may be found to have considerable native talent, and sooner or later becomes tabbed as an "underachiever." He gets as far as he does thanks in large measure to the high quality of his native intelligence, but he does not live up to the promise which others observe in him.

When this child grows up and enters a career, we may see the continuation of underachievement, marked by relative passivity and undistinguished performance. Where he may cast his lot is in the relative obscurity of group activity. Here he can bring his talents to bear in anonymous work. As soon as he becomes differentiated, he feels anxious and may seek to become immersed once again in group activity.

An important aspect of this pattern of response is the ingrained feeling that whatever the person undertakes is bound to fail. He does not feel quite whole and lacks a strong sense of identity. He is short on self-esteem and tends to quit before he starts in order to avoid confrontation with the fear that he might fail. Instead of risking failure he is willing to assume anonymity, hence the sense of resignation and sometimes fatigue which he communicates to those near to him.

A closer study of the dilemma surrounding the fear of failure indicates that the person has not resolved the concerns he has with competing. It may be that he has adopted or "internalized" unrealistic standards of performance or that he is competing internally with unreachable objects. Therefore he resolves to avoid the game because it is lost before it starts.

James Thurber's characterization of Walter Mitty provides a clear indication of this problem. Walter was a meek man who had difficulty in mobilizing himself for even the simplest tasks; yet in his inner world of fantasy, as Thurber portrays so humorously and touchingly, Walter Mitty is the grand captain of his destiny and the destiny of those who depend on him. He populates his inner world with images of himself as the pilot of an eight-engine bomber or the cool, skillful, nerveless surgeon who holds the life of his patient in his hands.

Fear of failure can be resolved only when the person is able to examine his inner competitive world, to judge its basis in reality, and to modify this structure in accordance with sensible standards.

Fear of Success

The fear of failure can be matched with its opposite, the fear of success. This latter pattern might be called the "Macbeth complex," since Shakespeare's play can be viewed symbolically for our purposes.

Macbeth was an ambitious man. The demon ambition was projected out in the form of the three witches and Macbeth's wife, who, Macbeth would lead us to believe, put the idea into his head to become king. But we do not believe for a minute that the ambition to become Number One existed anywhere but within Macbeth himself.

The crown rests uneasily on a tormented head. Macbeth is wracked with feelings of guilt for the misdeed he has committed —killing Duncan in order to become King—and then with uneasy suspicion. The guilt is easy enough for us to understand, but the suspicion is a bit more subtle. Macbeth presents himself to us as a character who committed a foul deed to attain an ambition and is then suspicious that others are envious of him and seek to displace him in the Number One position. So, there are few lieutenants to trust. And, paradoxically, the strongest subordinates become the ones least trusted and most threatening.

The play portrays in action the morbid cycle of the hostile-aggressive act followed by guilt and retribution. In addition, if we view the play symbolically, we can say that the individual, like Macbeth, may experience in fantasy the idea that one achieves position only through displacing someone else. Success, therefore, brings with it feelings of guilt and the urge to undo or to reverse the behavior that led to the success. If such concerns are strong enough—and they exist in all of us to some degree—then we may see implemented the fear of success.

The form of this implementation will vary. One prominent pattern it takes is in striving hard to achieve a goal, but just when the goal is in sight or within reach, the person sabotages himself. The self-sabotage can be viewed as a process of undoing—to avoid the success that may generate guilt. This process of self-sabotage is sometimes called snatching defeat out of the jaws of victory.

Theodore H. White in his book, *The Making of the President —1960*, conveys the impression that Nixon was undergoing the fear of success. There seemed to be too many errors of commission and omission to pass off the election simply in terms of external events and forces, important as these were.

MANAGING INNER CONFLICTS

We have called attention to the not easily accepted notion that conflicts of interest can and do exist within individuals and are not restricted to the relations among men in the ordinary conduct of affairs. The inner conflicts rooted in the emotional development of the individual are at the core of the leadership dilemma. It is misleading, in other words, to seek for causes of conflict exclusively in external forces.

Then, touching on a few of the inner conflicts of executives, they were grouped into two main types: (1) status anxiety, (2) competition anxiety. Both of these forms of inner conflict are rooted in the very process of human development in the strivings of individuals for some measure of autonomy and control over their environment. The forms happen to be especially crucial in the executive's world simply because he acts in the center of a network of authority and influence that at any point in time is subject to alteration. In fact, one can think of decision making and action in organizations as a continuing flow of influence interchanges where the sources of the power to influence are many. But whatever the external source through which any one person achieves power to influence, its final manifestations will reflect the inner emotional condition of the man.

Let us now see what guidelines exist for resolving and managing inner conflicts. There are six ideas to suggest here.

1. *The necessity of acknowledging and accepting the diversity of motivations.* The control of one's own responses and actions presupposes some accurate understanding of one's motivations. Everyone would like to believe that his inner world is populated only by the socially nice drives and wishes. But this is not the case. It is fruitless to attempt to deny awareness of the less acceptable, but equally human, feelings that we all experience, such as rivalry, dislike, rebelliousness, anger, and contempt. I am not urging executives to express these feelings impulsively. I am not of the school of thought that believes the catharsis of feelings in everyday relationships at work and at home is a good thing. But the awareness of how one is reacting in a situation is beneficial and permits more flexibility in thinking and action. Unless an executive establishes a close connection between his realms of thought and feeling, the two can exist in relative isolation from one another to the detriment of his effectiveness as a manager. At the very least, such self-estrangement involves considerable costs in the waste of energy.

2. *The necessity of establishing a firm sense of identity.* The exercise of leadership requires a strong sense of identity—knowing who one is and who one is not. The myth of the value of being an "all-around guy" is damaging to the strivings of an individual to locate himself from within and then to place himself in relation to others. This active location and placement of oneself prevents the individual from being defined by others in uncongenial terms. It prevents him also from being buffeted around the sea of opinions he must live within. A sense of autonomy, separateness, or identity permits a freedom of action and thinking so necessary for leadership.

Not the least significant part of achieving a sense of identity is the creative integration of one's past. There is no tailor who can convert a hayseed into a big-city boy—any more than a dude can become a cowboy for all the hours he spends on the range. Coming to terms with being a hayseed or a dude permits the development of a unique person who goes beyond the stereotypes offered to him as models.

3. *The necessity of maintaining constancy and continuity in response.* Closely related to the need for a sense of identity is a constancy in how one represents and presents himself to others. Constant alterations of oneself are confusing to work associates. These shifts are particularly damaging to subordinates who are entitled to the sense of security that comes from a feeling of reasonable continuity in the responses of their boss.

I knew of one group of executives, many of whom had the practice of taking tranquilizers before a meeting with the president of the company. They claimed that they needed the tranquilizers to help them withstand the angry reactions the president demonstrated when people acted as though they had not thought through the ideas they were presenting. They were mistaken. They used the tranquilizers because they were very unsure as to just what he would get angry about or when. If they had had some sense of the standards of performance to which he reacted kindly or harshly, they would have been able to spend less time worrying and more time working.

4. *The necessity of becoming selective in activities and relationships.* Most executives believe that gregariousness and participation in many activities at work and in the community are of great value in their life. In a sense this belief is true. But I would urge that greater attention needs to be paid to selectivity. Without carefully selecting the matters he gets involved in, the executive faces a drain on his emotional energy that can become quite costly. Selectivity implies the capacity to say "no" without the sense that one has lost esteem. The capacity to say "no" also implies that one is so constituted that he does not need esteem from diffuse persons and activities to enhance his self-worth.

5. *The necessity of learning to communicate.* Conflict resolution, both inner and external, depends on the capacities of men to communicate. Communication is a complex process and one that requires careful thought and attention. It requires a keen awareness of your own reactions, and it requires making your opinions

and attitudes known without wasteful delays. An unexpressed reaction that simmers and then boils within is apt to explode at inappropriate times; this may lead to increased confusion and concern in the minds of listeners.

6. *The necessity of living within a cyclical life pattern.* The effective utilization of energy seems to involve a rhythmic pattern of alternating between quite different modes or cycles of response. The prototype of alternating modes is probably best found in the comparison of wakefulness and sleep. Wakefulness suggests activity, conscious attention to problems, and the tension of concentration and action. Sleep is the epitome of passivity in the adult as well as in the child; here concerns are withdrawn from the outside world to a state of inner bliss. In this passive state the organism is rejuvenated and made ready for a new cycle of activity.

This prototype can be applied to a wide range of events in the daily life of the executive. Building oneself into a rhythmic pattern, whether it be around work or play, talking or listening, being at work alone or in association with others, may be essential for dealing with the strains of a difficult role.

SUMMING UP

Training oneself to act and react in the ways just discussed may sound like a formidable task. Formidable though it is, the basic necessity is to overcome the sense of inertia to which we are all susceptible from time to time. The most elementary step necessary for achieving a mature orientation as an executive is to assume responsibility for one's own development. Basic to this responsibility is the experiencing of oneself in the active mode. The sense of inertia referred to before is just the opposite; here life and events appear to occur apart from one's own intentions. As soon as an executive is able to assume responsibility for his own experience and in the course of doing so overcomes the sense of inertia, he is on the road toward experiencing leadership as an adventure in learning.

4 / The Dynamics of Subordinacy *

In December 1964, a thousand students of the University of California at Berkeley staged a sit-in demonstration in the main administration building. The next day, upon the orders of the Governor of the state, police forcibly removed and arrested the demonstrators. The student body retaliated with a campuswide strike, closing down the University's academic activities.

Responsible individuals everywhere were shocked by these events, including the apparent ineptness of the administration and the lack of communication between the authorities and the student body. Above all, the episode at Berkeley created all sorts of doubts about the responsibility and maturity of this new generation and its potential leaders.

For individuals in a position of authority the doubts activate opment and a potential for growth, because just how the individuals in junior positions in organizations respond to their relationship with authority figures. To be sure, the use of protest and demonstration on the part of students is a time-honored tradition in a free society. But even, or especially, protest and social reform must be carried out with a sense of the consequences of behavior. Above all, individuals who are the juniors in a vertical relationship have to avail themselves of the opportunities to learn

* Adapted from the article "The Dynamics of Subordinacy" in the May–June 1965 issue of the *Harvard Business Review* © 1965 by the President and Fellows of Harvard College, reprinted by permission.

from assessing consequences so that as they mature and assume increasing responsibilities their response to pressures will be seasoned by judgment and experience. Otherwise we face the prospect of a severe discontinuity in the quality of leadership in business and all segments of society.

For managers in business, the vexing problems of subordinacy are all too evident, leading frequently to paralysis on the part of authority figures.

A president of a large, aggressive concern came to me with an experience that had left him stunned by the unexpected behavior of subordinates at the junior levels. He had undertaken a program to select and train promising juniors for promotion to supervisory and staff jobs. He talked personally with many men and helped in the selection and preparation for promotion. The promotions were announced and were followed almost immediately by a wildcat strike led by dissatisfied subordinates who felt they had been overlooked.

What shocked the president was the fact that his intention to open new opportunities, to help people design for themselves a future in his organization, had misfired. He wondered where he had miscalculated the motivations of subordinates. He was on the verge of disillusionment with the younger generation.

This example from business is repeated in countless organization, although not necessarily with the visibility and dramatic impact of strikes and demonstrations. More subtle forms of the discontents of subordinacy are widespread. There is, for example, the individual who is unable to hold a job—who moves from one situation to the next expecting the grass to be greener elsewhere. The problem of "job hopping" is not restricted to any segment of society. One suspects, for example, that executive placement firms thrive on the discontents and illusions of persons who are willing perennially to live out of a suitcase.

The instances of sudden attitude reversal are equally instructive. Some individuals characteristically begin a relationship with authority figures by overidealizing their boss, overestimating his strengths and capabilities. There soon follows the opposite extreme of depreciation and underestimation. In listening to persons who polarize their feelings toward authority one soon becomes aware of the crucial role of their fantasy in creating and then destroying unrealistic images of other persons. The persistence of fantasy and the willingness of individuals to act upon it at the expense of reality attests to the strength of the emotional conflicts in subordinacy.

Another manifestation of the problems in subordinacy is the recurrence of defective work performances. I refer here to individuals who are unable to follow through on assignments, who display promise but fail to complete, who are excellent critics but faulty performers, who may be verbally adept but substantively inept.

Still another faulty condition of subordinacy is in the case of the highly dependent individual who accepts initiation but does not himself initiate. The amount of responsibility such persons assume reliably is quite limited. The fault in the relationship, frequently, is to count on a quality of initiative that psychologically is not available. The defect seems to be in little available energy for work and the absence of the capacity to tolerate visibility in performance. Instead, the trend is toward anonymity and compliance.

These symptoms of defective adaptations to the positions of subordinacy in organizations by no means exhaust the range of problems. Individuals on both sides of the vertical authority relationship could add countless other expressions of the difficulties in mastering the challenges and conflicts of the subordinate role.

But my purpose in this chapter is to go beyond the superficial symptoms to grasp the basic dynamics of subordinacy conflicts. Through understanding of the dynamics we may come to achieve greater sensitivity and judgment in this important aspect of human relationships. In turn we may learn to avoid the precipitous breaks in communication between authority and subordinates illustrated so dramatically and painfully in the events at Berkeley.

Subordinacy conflicts exist within the person as responses to inner tensions. These tensions usually lurk below the surface of conscious awareness but like a dormant volcano may erupt into patterns of behavior containing deep emotional content. And it is precisely this emotional intensity that overloads communications in the transactions between superior and subordinate.

In pursuing this underlying explanation of subordinacy conflicts I want to do three things here: (1) examine the psychological dimensions that assume prominence in the inner conflicts of the subordinate; (2) relate these inner conflicts to their origins in individual development; (3) suggest guidelines for individual and interpersonal resolutions of subordinacy conflicts.

DIMENSIONS OF THE INNER CONFLICTS IN SUBORDINACY

The eruption of subordinacy conflicts into behavior, whether through group-supported rebellion, or more individualistic actions, occurs as a response to the vertical relationship. This vertical relationship reflects and is reflected in the constellation of motives, wishes, and tensions within the individual himself. At the risk of oversimplifying, we can single out two trends in the constellation of motives for special attention.

One trend deals with the polar issue of *dominance and submission*. The potential conflict here is the balance achieved within the individual of his wishes to control and overpower the authority figures, and at the other extreme the equally strong wishes to be dominated and controlled by these same figures. The theme of dominance and submission achieves a unity in meaning because both extremes aim at a single outcome: to secure the sole possession of figures who regulate and dispense the life sustaining rewards and punishments. This aim accounts for the intensity of reactions in the subordinacy role, since the game is real and the stakes high. In the case of business organizations, the stakes are often related to chances for promotion and career success.

The second trend relates to the balance achieved between *activity and passivity* in the individual's characteristic patterns of behavior. At the extremes, the position may yield very active modes of response. Here the individual initiates and intrudes into his environment. At the other extreme, the individual characteristically waits to be initiated upon and behaves in response to the stimulation from outside himself. The active-passive modes are usually well established as character traits of the individual, having special significance in his personal economy. The personal economy reflects the tensions of reward and deprivation, of energy expended and gratifications realized, of risks in frustration and the need to defend against these risks.

Patterns of Subordinacy

We can use the combination of these two trends to describe four patterns of subordinacy, particularly to illustrate types of inner conflict (see Figure 1). At the extremes, the dominant-active (Type A) represents the Impulsive; dominant-passive (Type B), the Compulsive; submissive-active (Type C), the Masochistic; and submissive-passive (Type D), the Withdrawn. Closer examination of each type with suitable illustrations will clarify the patterns of behavior and response involved.

1. *The Impulsive Subordinate:* The main feature of subordinacy that aims to dominate relationships with authority figures through active means is rebellion. The effort is to overthrow authority and flout its symbols usually with the unconscious significance of displacing the father.

This theme of rebellion is evident in the group formations of adolescence but can continue for a long time beyond this period of life. In work situations certain forms of rebellion lead to the inability to hold a job and diffused conflict with superiors. Other forms of rebellion are more constructive in the sense that they overcome complacency and the status quo.

In a study of interpersonal relations and job satisfaction that I conducted in the mid-1950s, I observed the nature of overt rebellion and its significance.[1] One of the workers, a highly gifted

[1] See A. Zaleznik, *Worker Satisfaction and Development* (Cambridge: Division of Research, Harvard Business School, 1956).

individual, taunted his supervisor by placing notices on the bulletin board that demanded to know why certain kinds of tools were unavailable in the shop. The notices quoted authorities who recommended these tools and after each quotation there followed a challenge to the supervisor and the management as a whole.

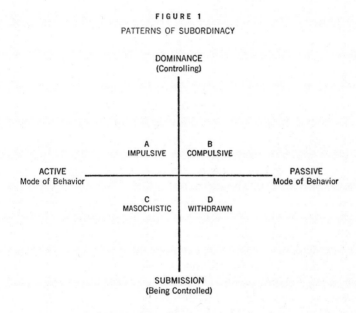

FIGURE 1
PATTERNS OF SUBORDINACY

Subsequently the supervisor forbade the posting of notices. The employee took this as a challenge and built a private bulletin board near his work bench on which he continued to post notices. One day the supervisor called the employee to talk to him. The employee became rude, told his supervisor "to go to hell," and found himself fired.

Inquiry into his situation indicated a history of job hopping. In fact this employee told me he expected to be fired, "that it always happens." This mechanism of predicting dire events in the future stands as a "self-fulfilling" prophecy. The individual makes a reality out of a fantasy through his own behavior.

The fantasy involved in this case includes the struggle with powerful authority figures in which the subject ultimately loses, but only as a means of escaping from authority. The job hopping can be viewed as impulsive action to break off contact where the fantasy of the struggle becomes too painful to endure.

The overt aim is to dominate through activity; but beneath this aim is the fear of taking control. This mechanism explains partially why rebels frequently have difficulty controlling and managing affairs even when they assume power. The process of rebellion as an expression of a fantasy is significant. The fantasy relates to prowess like the story of David and Goliath; a seemingly weak individual overpowers a much stronger opponent to assume control and dominance. But in real life such fantasies usually result in injury and frustration to the hero.

The impulse to act can therefore be seen in both its outer form as very aggressive behavior and in its inner meaning as a fantasy involving a rivalrous situation.

In the illustration of the rebel, further indications of its dynamics become evident when we understand the painful loneliness implicit in much of impulsive behavior. The rebel may very much want to be close to others but finds such closeness difficult to sustain because of interfering fantasies of being dominated and controlled by others. The employee just described lived a lonely existence as a middle-aged bachelor with no friends. He enjoyed one activity: chess competition. He was a gifted player and this in itself is revealing because it indicated that his main human relationships existed within a ritual of combat in the two-person relationship: of victor and vanquished.

While describing impulsiveness and rebellion as defective aspects of subordinacy, it would be a mistake to see only this side of the coin. When the impulsive individual assumes control of his fantasies, highly constructive behavior appears. Take the spontaneous and courageous subordinate as an example. He may use rebellion to speak frankly and assert his views in discussions of work problems. He avoids compliance and conformity, not only out of impatience but also out of the urge to create and achieve. This constructive use of dominance and activity makes it possible for individuals in the position of subordinate to influence events. They are highly appreciated by strong authority figures who themselves tire of endless experiences with "yes men."

But the line between impulsiveness as constructive and destructive character traits is difficult to draw. Similar dynamics underlie both; the difference, however, resides in the degree of individual self-control. The constructive rebel knows how to use his urge to dominate and acts in appropriate ways. The destructive rebel exerts no self-control and finds himself dominated by his own fantasies.

2. *The Compulsive Subordinate:* Compulsive subordinacy aims to secure dominance and control, but through passive means.

The dictionary distinction between compulsiveness and impulsiveness often leads to confusion between two psychologically different characteristics. Whereas the impulsive type acts without thinking, the compulsive type acts under the effects of overelaborated thought processes indicating a powerful conscience and strong guilt feelings.

Compulsiveness leads to rigid behavior that seeks to expiate guilt through a number of mechanisms. The individual who acts but then reverses himself out of a sense of uncertainty is often dominated by guilt. Or the person who is indecisive, who can only think in endless riddles but cannot reach conclusions is also operating under the burden of guilt.

The guilt is connected with the wish to dominate and control authority figures; the hesitation, doubt, and rigidity are connected with the defense against these wishes and the force of conscience that exacts so much pressure on the individual. The origin of the wishes, the guilt, and the primitive conscience are tied to the early experiences of the individual.

Compulsiveness has a strange and intriguing quality about it, largely resulting from its use of passive behavior to control situations. Passivity consists of indirect and manipulative attempts at influence where the actor himself may be unaware of the aim of his behavior. The clearest illustration of control through passivity is in the case of the hypochondriac. All indications point to illness and suffering as an experience that the victim endures passively. Yet the effect, as members of the hypochondriac's family know, is to control the behavior of those close to the "victim." The entire family experience may be organized to meet the needs of the victim and in point of fact this is the unconscious wish underlying much of the suffering. The restrictions the victim lives by become the controls that dominate the lives of others. In other words, "misery loves company" but by unconscious design rather than by accident.

The hypochondriac's behavior presents an extreme and clear instance of control through passive means. But compulsiveness exists in more subtle forms. The following case example illustrates this quality of compulsiveness, especially the features of doubt, attitude reversal, and hidden aggression combined with denial of responsibility.

Dr. Richard Dodds, a physics research worker, entered the office and showed his superior, Dr. Blackman, a letter. This letter was from another research institution, offering Dodds a position. Blackman read the letter.

Dodds: "What do you think of that?"

Blackman: "I knew it was coming. He asked me if it would be all right if he sent it. I told him to go ahead, if he wanted to."

Dodds: "I didn't expect it, particularly after what you said to me last time (*pause*). I'm really quite happy here. I don't want you to get the idea that I am thinking of leaving. But I thought I should go and visit him—I think he expects it—and I wanted to let you know that just because I was thinking of going down, that didn't mean I was thinking of leaving here, unless of course, he offers me something extraordinary."

Blackman: "Why are you telling me all this?"

Dodds: "Because I didn't want you hearing from somebody else that I was thinking of leaving here because I was going for a visit to another institution. I really have no intention of leaving here you know, unless he offers me something really extraordinary that I can't afford to turn down. I think I'll tell him that, that I am willing to look at his laboratory, but unless there is something unusual for me, I have no intention of leaving here."

Blackman: "It's up to you."

Dodds: "What do you think?"

Blackman: "Well, what? About what? You've got to make up your mind."

Dodds: "I don't consider too seriously this job. He is not offering anything really extraordinary. But I *am* interested in what he had to say, and I would like to look around his lab."

Blackman: "Sooner or later you are going to have to make up your mind where you want to work."

Dodds replied sharply: "That depends on the offers, doesn't it?"

Blackman: "No, not really; a good man always gets offers. You get a good offer and you move, and as soon as you have moved, you get other good offers. It would throw you into confusion to consider all the good offers you will receive. Isn't there a factor of how stable you want to be?"

Dodds: "But I'm not shopping around. I already told you that. He sent me this letter, I didn't ask him to. All I said was I think I should visit him, and to you that's shopping around."

Blackman: "Well, you may choose to set aside your commitment here if he offers you something better. All I am saying is that you will still be left with the question of you've got to stay some place, and where is that going to be?"

The discussion continued on how it would look if Dodds changed jobs at this point and finally Dodds said:

Dodds: "Look, I came in here, and I want to be honest with you, but you go and make me feel all guilty, and I don't like that."

Blackman: "You are being honest as can be."

Dodds: "I didn't come in here to fight. I don't want to disturb you."

Blackman: "I'm not disturbed. If you think it is best for you to go somewhere else, that is O.K. with me."

Again there is a lengthy exchange about what does Dodds really want and how would his leaving look to others. Finally Dodds blurts out:

Dodds: "I don't understand you. I came in here to be honest with you, and you make me feel guilty. All I wanted was to show you this letter, and let you know what I was going to do. What should I have told you?"

Blackman: "That you had read the letter, and felt that under the circumstances it was necessary for you to pay a visit to the professor, but that you were happy here, and wanted to stay at least until you had got a job of work done."

Dodds: "I can't get over it. You think there isn't a place in the world I'd rather be than here in this lab. . . ."

In introducing this case illustration, I suggested we watch especially for four qualities of compulsiveness in the behavior of the person in the subordinate position. These qualities are: (1) doubt; (2) attitude reversal; (3) hidden aggression; (4) denial of responsibility.

The theme of *doubt* appears throughout the entire interchange, reminiscent in many ways of Hamlet's obsessional doubting. Instead of "to be or not to be," the doubting in this illustration centers on the dilemma of career: where and when does one "settle in" and forgo imaginary (or half-real) opportunities? Every person launching his career is susceptible to hesitation and concern over opportunities lost. In work, as in marriage, lingering thoughts over the "other person" or the "other job" intrude into the optimism that accompanies fresh experience. Where other individuals stake a claim on a career, then pursue their line of work, the compulsive individual continues to doubt. As in the preceding case, he even titillates his environment to keep the doubting alive.

The stubbornness underlying the compulsive doubting is suggested again and again in the example by the inability or unwillingness of the subordinate to "hear" direct advice on the importance of ending doubt and undertaking work.

Attitude reversal consists of rapid oscillation between positive and negative feelings in human encounters. In the preceding case, the subordinate would not think of leaving the laboratory, "unless, of course, he offers me something extraordinary." The technical term for attitude reversal is ambivalence, suggesting the simultaneous influence of both positive and negative emotions toward a single object or event. It goes hand-in-hand with doubting and together they serve to maintain a steady level of tension in the individual's human relationships and work activity.

The third theme, *hidden aggression*, is unavoidably present in an otherwise passive pattern of behavior. The hidden aggression appears in the illustration in such accusing comments as: "All I said was I think I should visit him and to you that's shopping around." Despite disclaimers like, "I didn't come here to fight. I don't want to disturb you," the underlying intention is to provoke arguments and verbal tugs-of-war. This underlying motive resides in the uneasy balance between dependent and independent wishes frequently at the core of conflict in the compulsive subordinate.

The fourth theme is *denial of responsibility*. If one detects a note of frustration in supervisors who work with compulsive subordinates, it is because of the tendency to get impaled on the horns of the dilemma upon which the subordinate rides. Doubting, attitude reversals, and hidden aggression are ordinarily tough to take, but the "last straw" presents itself in the denial of responsibility.

The case evidenced this theme most poignantly in the subordinate's statement at the end: "I don't understand you. I came in here to be honest with you, and you make me feel guilty." This states the essence of dominance through passivity—that conflict, problems, and nasty emotions exist in the outer world and are infused from without rather than generated from within.

Much of the literature on management calls for authority with responsibility. Of equal importance is the need for subordinacy with responsibility, a kind of response absent in the compulsive pattern just described.

3. *The Masochistic Subordinate:* Masochism consists of the quest for pleasure through the endurance of pain. True masochism is a serious emotional disturbance, but it also exists as a trace element in the character structure of individuals. In the case of

the subordinate who demonstrates the desire for pain, it is an active attempt to submit to the control and assertiveness of the authority figure. Here again this particular dynamic of subordinacy is to be understood as an aspect of unconscious motivation.

The pattern of subordinacy that seeks to evoke aggression from an authority figure is basically a means for guarding against one's own aggressive tendencies. The individual fears his own aggression and the prospect that once he begins to show aggression his destructive potential will get beyond his control. Instead of hurting others, he hurts himself through provoking others. The aim is self-destructive.

The most common manifestation of this pattern of subordinacy is in the case of the accident-prone employee: he may mean to get mad at his boss, as a representative of authority, but only hurts himself through lapses of attention or by taking undue risks. A side effect of this self-punishing behavior is to evoke sympathy and attention from others. At the same time, it invites control from others and the abdication of personal responsibility.

A more subtle form of masochistic traits in work behavior is the initiation of disparagement through less than effective performance. The individual invites criticism and shaming by sheer inadequacies in his output. The explanation for these inadequacies does not lie in ability, experience, or even lack of hard work. All of these attributes for good performance may be present; but they are not utilized and directed because to perform well means to accept praise and responsibility when the underlying motivation is to endure persecution and shame at the hands of an imagined aggressor.

We observe, from time to time, individuals in organizations who "identify with the underdog"; they are quick to see injustice in the actions of authority figures and sense oppression in the lives of others who have little power and influence. Apart from the realities of oppression and the existence of the "underdog," the identification with the helpless and weak against the powerful and the strong reflects this masochistic bent in personality.

Subordinates who reflect this tendency act sometimes like an older son in the family who takes the side of the younger siblings against imagined oppressive actions of parents. This type of subordinate suffers vicariously, and perhaps simultaneously finds an outlet for pent-up aggression. The target is the oppressor, who stands in the place of parents as the original authority figures.

It is very useful to attack oppressors, but the problem is in seeing oppression where none exists. Instances when standards of performance are enforced in an equitable way may be attacked as vehemently as arbitrary discipline. Discrimination in judging real from imagined inequity is absent in the individual who organizes his experience around identification with the oppressed.

It is worth repeating to suggest that the theme of aggressive behavior while identifying with the underdog serves the aim of becoming a target of attack from powerful authority figures. Submission is the sought-after end, while the active-aggressive behavior is the means.

One hears periodically of the employee who commits a crime, such as embezzling funds or taking personal "kick-backs" on purchase contracts, of which no one thought him capable. A trusted employee with a fine record suddenly steals; and from the way the act is committed it appears that the culprit wants to make certain the violation will be discovered and punished. This puzzling behavior becomes less difficult to understand if it is viewed as a masochistic act. The personal sense of guilt of the masochistic employee leads him to act without thinking and to bring punishment down upon himself. The sense of guilt usually has little direct relation to realistic aspects of the individual's life in a work situation. Its roots lie elsewhere.

I mean to emphasize here the point that the masochistic pattern, as with the other extremes, continues a dynamic that originated in the early years of experience. The hidden desire to endure suffering at the hands of a powerful aggressor recreates the infantile wishes used to solve, although tenuously, the dilemmas of early development. It is remarkable to observe the degree to which history repeats itself in the life of the individual. The repetition, however, does not occur through impersonal forces or the whims of chance, but rather through inadequate mastery of inner conflicts.

One way of responding intelligently to the provocations of the masochistic personality is to avoid the game. The masochistic subordinate seeks pleasure in becoming the target of aggression. Avoidance of aggressive response can break the cycle and return the issue to the place where it belongs; within the individual himself. In this sense avoidance of the reciprocal (the sadistic response to masochistic provocation) holds open the possibility for learning lessons from experience.

4. *The Withdrawn Subordinate:* It will help in concluding this description of four patterns of subordinacy to remind ourselves of the basic dimensions from which the patterns have been established. I suggested that one dimension in the continuing development of the individual from infancy through the career years is control. Here the polar issues of dominance and submission, in controlling and being controlled, exist in the fantasy and thinking process both conscious and unconscious. The problem of control exists, so to speak, inside the skin of the person. It is not therefore obvious or easily described from the outside.

Fantasies about control range in the extreme from a sense of omnipotence in relation to the environment, to the complete expectation that forces outside the self determine one's destiny. The range is from a kind of pathological insertion of oneself into all manner of events and circumstances to the absence of any area in which will and direction can have some influence over one's own activity and the environment.

In speaking of control over the environment I refer not only to inanimate forces but also to the significant world of other persons. It is here, in the realm of human relationships, that the issue of control cuts most deeply.

What the individual had done to him, in reality and fantasy, becomes the foundations for the later attitudes toward figures both of love and of authority at work and in the family.

The second dimension in this analytic structure is the distribution of active and passive components in the individual's behavior patterns. Activity and passivity are important elements of character structure. An observer watching someone act in relation to others becomes aware of a patterned response—the observed person for example may take the active-aggressive stance. He initiates, directs, and asserts himself in the situation. Or, in the opposite case of passivity, the individual waits, responds to others, is quiet, and shows little or no emotional reaction.

These character traits are readily observable. But to a surprising extent, individuals are themselves quite unaware that their style or mode of action is so patterned and consistent. If someone should describe their mode of behavior, they might be interested, but also taken aback.

The reason for this seeming paradox—that what others can see clearly is anything but obvious to the person himself—is in the very nature of character.

The dimension of activity-passivity is, of course, an oversimplified way of talking about complex behavioral acts. But it will do for our purposes. In observing individuals interacting with their environment one can differentiate between two extremes. The active consists of a pattern of initiation or outward thrust. The individual stimulates the environment by directing energy outward. The passive mode consists mainly of low energy directed outward. Behavior is in *response* to stimulation from others.

The combination of the two dimensions of inner motivation and external behavior establishes the four patterns of subordinacy: (1) the impulsive (dominant-active); (2) the compulsive (dominant-passive); (3) the masochistic (submissive-active), and finally; (4) the withdrawn (submissive-passive).

In the descriptions and interpretations of these patterns I have emphasized the more extreme representations. I have also tried to present a process rather than, necessarily, a particular person. While individuals in the role of subordinate usually tend toward one or the other of the four patterns, they are not rigidly fixed in a category. There is a measure of flexibility and variation depending on the person's dispositions, the time, place, and particular individuals with whom relationships develop.

The fourth pattern, withdrawal, represents an outcome of successively turning interest and attention from the outer world toward oneself. The individual invests his emotional resources relatively speaking in his fantasies after having withdrawn them from other persons.

The pattern is a form of submission because the individual no longer cares about the orientation and content of his work. His behavioral mode is passive in that energy from within is released only sparingly.

This picture of withdrawal through passive submission is in its extreme form a serious human disability that comes about because of lack of trust. The world is seen as malevolent and ungiving; therefore the individual withdraws investment in it. But even in its less severe forms, withdrawal presents a difficult problem in superior-subordinate relationships. The subordinate's lack of trust, interest, and involvement makes him unsusceptible to influence. He acquiesces and does what he is told, but without orientation and interest. He contributes little to interchange and thinking necessary for innovative work. He may handle routine tasks well enough, but little beyond the necessary demands of his work.

The withdrawn subordinate presents other paradoxical features. In many cases, he appears loyal and accepting of existing standards. To illustrate, in a current study of professional scientists and engineers in a research and development center my colleagues and I discovered a type of career adjustment with features similar to the withdrawal pattern described here. Over an interval of about two years during which we collected data, no individual classified in this group left the company. All other groups had a small, but readily apparent turnover rate, including some individuals who left because they were dissatisfied with the work and others who left for better opportunities elsewhere.

The apathy evident in the absence of any turnover was supported by further evidence. There existed, for example, an interesting contradiction in response. On the one hand, the withdrawn type expressed personal disappointment in his career, a feeling of fatigue, presumably neurotic in origin, some anxiety and depression. On the other hand, individuals in this group tended to evaluate favorably their company, supervisor, and work colleagues. They expressed little desire to move elsewhere or to seek opportunities in other types of work.

Unlike some points of view that attribute withdrawal and apathy to oppressive conditions in the organization's authority structure, the evidence supports the view that its genesis lay in the individual's developmental history. This history includes a perception of a passive-withdrawn father, a cold, hostile mother with the consequence of marked inability to mobilize and use constructively aggressive impulses. The withdrawal and apathy are themselves a consequence, along with depression, of the turning of aggression inward. Such a pattern does not originate by and large in an external situation. It resides in the fantasies and wishes in the individual's unconscious.

Subordinacy and Individual Development

As I suggested earlier, the problems experienced in subordinate positions are usually the end product of a long historical process. Developmental experience within the successive stages of the life cycle, particularly in the family, lay down the basic patterns of subordinacy.

Adolescence and Subordinacy Conflicts

The direct and conscious confrontation with the problems of authority and subordinacy usually occur during the adolescent stage of development. This period is fraught with pain and anxiety for parents and adolescent alike. And much of the playout of subordinacy conflicts in the business organization represents the prolongation or continuation of the adolescent life crises.

The essential task of adolescence is to achieve independence from the family and assume the responsibilities of the adult. This task, in reality, is never fully completed, yet we usually acknowledge its completion when the individual begins his work career, marries, and becomes the head of a family.

The difficulty in adolescence stems from the presence of opposite forces within the personality. There is both a "push" toward rapid maturation for which the person may feel inadequately prepared and a "pull" toward the earlier securities in the close relationships with the parents. Yet the pull has to be overcome or there would be little basis for severing the old ties and establishing the new ones of adulthood.

This simultaneous push and pull within the personality accounts for much of the bizarre quality of adolescent behavior. The individual himself, let alone those who care for him, may not know whether to respond to the push of development or to the pull of security and comfort within the family circle. Both aspects have to be defended against until they have been assimilated within the personality.

To make matters even more difficult for the developing adult, the crisis of adolescence reawakens and reactivates a series of conflicts of the earlier stages of development. We owe a great deal to psychoanalytic psychology for revealing the dynamics of development from birth onward, especially in its demonstration of the importance of the infancy years. Of particular importance here is the reactivation during adolescence of the *conflicts of intimacy* in the relationship between mother and child, and the *conflicts of initiative* in the triangle of mother, father, and child.

Conflicts of Intimacy

The "pull" confronting the adolescent is toward a restoration of the primary love and dependency relationship with the mother. During the earliest period of development, well before the capacity of the child to use words and concepts, all of his life-giving needs were secured in the intimacy of the primary pairing with his mother or some substitute figure. In many ways, this initial intimacy prepares the child for the experience of intimacy as an adult, but it contains danger as well.

The danger comes from two sources: (1) the experience of separation; (2) the desire to restore the paradise lost. Separation from the primary relationship of intimacy usually generates considerable anger and even rage. This anger must somehow be dissipated and channeled into constructive ends during development; otherwise, it remains as a destructive potential within one of the four patterns of subordinacy described earlier. Closely related to the separation problem that is reactivated during adolescence is the desire to restore the original state of intimacy, the regressive "pull" that acts so strongly on the developing individual. If the pull becomes strong enough, and the individual gives in to it, he may remain markedly dependent all his life and unable to take the steps necessary for mature adulthood in work and family.

Evidence of the strength of the "pull" toward restoration of the earlier security is available in adult disturbances such as alcoholism, depression, and stomach ulcers. These symptoms in the adult guard against the rage and anger as well as reflect the desire for the primary intimacy relationship. The "angry young man" theme of contemporary novels and films such as "Saturday Night and Sunday Morning" or "This Sporting Life" are good reflections of the problems posed by the pull toward passivity in the male.

Let me repeat that the origins of subordinacy conflicts as they appear in work organizations reside in the process of development. These conflicts come into visible focus during adolescence, one aspect of which is the conflict of intimacy, or the longing for the security and warmth once experienced in the closeness of the mother-infant relationship.

Conflicts of Initiative

Another significant arena for conflict is over the possibility for initiative and the competitive potential. This conflict is also reawakened during adolescence and represents the imagined dangers in the "push" toward maturation. Here again, the problem is not experienced for the first time during adolesence but is instead a reactivation of earlier dilemmas in development. In this case, the dilemma is spun out in the structure of the triangle of mother-father-child. The relevance of the triangle in all life situations is fashioned along the lines of the early rivalry for supremacy, the desire to be Number One.

Sigmund Freud noted the importance of the triangle in observations of emotionally disturbed patients who appeared anxious, guilt-ridden, and dominated by undefined fears of attacking and being attacked. He correlated the adult disturbances with a conflict in infancy occurring between the ages of three and six—"the Oedipus complex." The triangle in Sophocles' Greek tragedy consisted of Oedipus, his mother, and his father. Having killed his father, married his mother unknowingly, and became the king, Oedipus was punished by being blinded and cast out.

Studies of normal as well as pathological human development indicate the fact that the oedipal period is a common growth phase. The young male child has a strong longing for the sole possession of his mother and treats his father as a rival. The longing and rivalry are contained for the most part in fantasy and play activities of the child. But their strength and significance should not be underestimated.

The child while experiencing the longing and rivalry is aware of the superior strength of the father and fears retaliation for his wishes. This fear springs from the tendency of the child to attribute or project his own inner fantasies onto the father. This attribution becomes a feeding ground for anxiety; when strong enough it becomes displaced in the form of phobias and related anxiety symptoms. Among the most important symptoms are work inhibitions, the inability to exert initiative and to perform.

The Oedipus complex is initially resolved in the capacity of the child to test reality through the eyes of loving parents. He identifies with his rival and delays the gratification of infantile wishes: "If I cannot substitute for father, I will try to be like him." This formula for identification becomes the dynamic for subsequent development including the capacity to learn and assume, at an appropriate stage in life, the position of a responsible man.

But it would be a mistake to view the Oedipus complex as a piece of finished business at the time the child enters school. For many individuals the issue is not so simply resolved and may lead to a frozen position in the developmental tasks of life or to a retreat to an earlier stage of development. Even without marked failures in the mastery of the Oedipus complex one finds the reopening of the classic problem of the triangle during subordinacy crises of adolescence and adulthood.

The individual functions in the role of subordinate through much of the adolescent and career years. The oedipal strivings may continue to exert a strong pull toward immature behavior and account for many of the problems of subordinacy that we observe in everyday life. The overanxious subordinate, the poor performer, the indecisive man—these and other types of personality conflicts involving subordinacy reflect the impact of the Oedipus complex.

The Gains of Development

The conflicts of intimacy and initiative are inherent in the process of development. They are not to be viewed as negative experiences by themselves, since all development from infancy onward takes place within a matrix of conflicting forces—the push toward maturity and the pull toward restitution of earlier gratifying situations. Instead, the main test of development is in the kind and degree of learning through inner conflict.

The objective of learning remains central to our interest in resolving the conflicts of subordinacy. And with this idea in mind, let us turn to the conclusions of this chapter.

CONCLUSION

There are two points of view involved in resolving subordinacy conflicts. The first is the position of the individual in the midst of personal subordinacy conflicts. The second is the point of view of the authority figure who is on the other side of the vertical relationship. Those who exercise authority in relation to other individuals may wonder how they can help to minimize these conflicts and help their subordinates in their efforts to grow and mature.

Actually, these two points of view are interrelated. In examining the personal and interpersonal problems of any individual in an organization, it is impressive to note the fact that no one is ever separated from the role of subordinate, no matter how high his position in the hierarchy. Everyone has some authority figure whose evaluations and responses are of great personal significance. Simultaneously, however, there are subordinates who look to this same person for direction, guidance, and evaluation.

The fact that authority and subordinacy conflicts exist within a web of human relationships does not minimize the importance for the individual of learning to assume responsibility for his own behavior. Whether looking at the relationship from above or below, the person has to learn to separate his reactions from those of other persons and to achieve appropriate self-management. This attitude of self-management contradicts the tendency to attribute blame to others for the personal predicaments of immediate experience.

One important practical implication of self-management is the awareness of how frequently one tries to relieve old conflicts from the past in the present. All too frequently bosses in organizations duplicate the shadowy father figures from the past and are used as objects for the transfer of unresolved conflicts. The subordinate should learn to recognize his tendency to overload present relationships in terms of personal history and to mediate and govern his reactions so that they accord with reality. It is unrealistic, for example, to overidealize one's boss just as it is usually unrealistic to depreciate his authority and competence.

Superior and subordinate alike can experience considerable help in viewing the conflicts of subordinacy as conditions of development. Subordinates in fact do learn from experience provided they are not excessively overburdened with the unfinished business of the past relationships with their parents. Where there are abundant indications that past has taken over the present reality, then it pays to understand that by and large little change can occur within the superior-subordinate work relationship.

The superior is not in a position to act as therapist for his subordinates. He should not try, but he should be sufficiently knowledgeable to sort out realistic issues within his work relationships from the neurotic conflicts of personal development. This distinction removes the edge of guilt from human relationships in work situations and frequently serves to remove much of the static that impedes communication.

The realistic issues in work relationships include differences in objectives, and in ways of realizing mutually desirable goals. Neurotic conflicts of the past intrude upon reality of the present. In one superior-subordinate relationship, for example, the subordinate always seemed to discover problems that sounded real indeed. But upon discussing them, at his own initiative, with his boss, he would typically end on a reassuring note—that the problems of meeting production schedules will be overcome and that the boss should not worry. Closer examination of these repetitive interactions initiated by the subordinate showed its purpose in seeking reassurances that he was an effective and dependable person. As always, such thinly disguised efforts at reassurance seldom reassure because the authority figure ends up questioning the judgment of the subordinate while unable to satisfy an overwhelming self-generated need for approval.

Both superior and subordinate can learn from experience when they are reasonably free from past conflicts. Growth and change do occur but only very slowly, and more readily for those individuals who are building on a strong foundation of personal competence. In contrast to the theme of learning through experience, we must face the prospect of certain individuals requiring a re-education, where the lessons learned in the past obstruct the capacity to function in the present. This re-education takes place best within a professional relationship, and it is usually wise to seek out a specialist in psychoanalysis and psychiatry for such help.

In terms of seeking guidelines to govern the transactions within superior-subordinate relationship, there are several ideas worth pondering.

1. *Know your own mind:* It is important for both superior and subordinate to know where one stands on issues of work or personal conflict. We usually hear that it is important to listen to the other person and understand his point of view. This is good advice as far as it goes. What gets left out to the misfortune of all concerned is the fact that competent behavior depends on the ability of the individual to know where he stands and what he would like to see happen. In particular, the authority figure may find himself tyrannized by his own vacillations. If the subordinate is confused and torn by mixed feelings, it will do him little good to find his boss equally confused. In this sense, knowing where one stands and being prepared to take a position has a salutary effect on human relationships.

2. *Avoid the disabling reciprocal:* In every interpersonal relationship there is usually a balancing effect that takes place. A particular pattern of behavior of, say, the subordinate implies a reciprocal pattern of behavior on the part of the superior. If one individual talks, the reciprocal role necessary to balance the transaction is that of the listener. The relationship is unbalanced in this case if both individuals talk at the same time.

A balanced relationship is not always desirable. It is especially undesirable to play the reciprocal to one of the four patterns of conflicted subordinacy. Each of these patterns tends to evoke a kind of reciprocal response that reinforces the conflict and that creates a vicious circle. The masochistic subordinate seeks to evoke aggression and punishment. Avoidance of this reciprocal response breaks the transaction and requires rethinking as a prelude to change.

A reciprocal may in some cases be the opposite behavior; in other cases, the reciprocal is a similar response. For example, the compulsive doubter evokes doubt and guilt in others as the reciprocal response. The avoidance of the reciprocal in this case means to present a firm and decisive stance to break the chain of doubt.

The reciprocal cannot be avoided if the individual pondering these guidelines for behavior is a poor observer of human interaction and emotion. To choose, or to avoid, the reciprocal with intelligence requires the ability to observe and understand human behavior. A good place to start cultivating this ability is in reading accurately one's own behavior.

3. *Watch for the resonance effect:* There is a strong tendency in human relationships for individuals to experience the feelings that others have in the course of face-to-face interactions. In this sense we tend to resonate in response to the feeling tones originating in other persons. In the positive, resonance may yield the quality of empathy, or the capacity to sense what is going on in the other person. There is also a negative to resonance that is worth watching.

In no case should the origins of emotions be confused. The compulsive subordinate lives with guilt and, buy the process of resonance, tends to generate guilt in others. Trouble can be avoided when one identifies the resonance effect and clearly separates the origin of the feeling from one's own reactions. Once the sources of the feelings are properly located, the individual is free to respond in terms of his own evaluation of what is needed. The freedom of response provokes rethinking and learning as opposed to the deadly repetitive patterns encountered so frequently in superior-subordinate relationships.

4. *Objectify conflict:* When conflict arises in superior-subordinate relationships a potential for deterioration arises. It is not useful to increase this potential by dealing with the emotional bases of the conflict head on. For one thing, it may not be at all clear in the minds of the individuals concerned just what the emotional factors are. For another, the emotions may be too painful to bring into the transaction.

The possibility of deterioration is minimized if ways can be found to objectify the conflict. When a senior is dissatisfied with the behavior of his subordinate, it is of little help to criticize personality characteristics, or to propose changes in character traits. It can, however, help a great deal for the supervisor to discuss particular aspects of performance closely related to the job. Here issues are broken down into components and procedures are discovered for dealing with them. The size and scope of the conflict is reduced to manageable proportions as ways are found for exploring particular concerns. The effort, in other words, is directed toward partial answers rather than toward the heroic attempt to solve total conflicts once and for all.

5. *Identify and address the reality:* Work relationships are governed and judged in the final analysis by their contributions to purposes. There are always present, therefore, reality issues to which attention can be addressed. The purpose of superior-subordinate relationships in most organizations is to identify reality concerns, those problems that require solutions to move the organization closer to its goals.

The orientation to reality does not require coldness or insensitivity. On the contrary the search for reality problems can be conducted with considerable enthusiasm and regard for feelings. But at the same time, warmth and sensitivity are not substitutes for problem solving and other attempts at dealing with reality.

6. *Maintain contact:* There are times in organizations when the going gets tough for authority figures and subordinates alike. The temptation to withdraw is great during these painful experiences. As a temporary measure, withdrawal may be quite necessary. But it fails as a permanent stance. Withdrawal to nurse one's sense of having been injured is the point at issue here. There is also a kind of constructive withdrawal that is prelude to forming and consolidating a new position.

Withdrawal in the face of injury breaks contact with reality. If the withdrawal persists fantasy can take over leading to a whole host of incorrect ideas about the situation in which one finds himself. It leads to difficulty in introducing the corrective mechanisms associated with learning, particularly where authority relations are concerned. There are many ways known to all of us to maintain contact in the face of injury. The main problem is to avoid the temptation of withdrawal when it is unconstructive.

In reviewing and thinking about these guidelines for resolving the conflicts of subordinacy, one principle stands out. This is the need for superior and subordinate alike to recognize the truth when they see it. I refer here not to abstract truth, but to the concrete reality of that which exists in human relationships. Before change can occur in self and others, recognition must be given to the reality. It is here that observation and understanding play a very important role in human relationships. It is in this sense that description and explanation of patterns of subordinacy can be useful to both sides of the authority transactions in modern organizations.

5 / Equality and the Problem of Rivalry

John Gardner in his book *Excellence*,[1] asked if our society can be equal and excellent at the same time. The question can be put directly to leaders in business and industry. As business grows larger and assumes to increasing degrees the features of bureaucracy with its so-called rational procedures of management, is it possible to recognize and reward excellence without engendering the feelings connected with inequality and special privilege?

All of us have encountered administrators whose primary role conception is the maintenance of harmony within their organization. These administrators appear especially sensitive to the question of equality. They try hard to assure equal treatment to persons within the organization. The suggestion of special treatment engenders the fear that major discontents will be stirred up and, indeed, there is good evidence to indicate that the faintest indications of *singularization* stir the deepest passions of resentment in the minds of men.

Yet the paradox remains that men are not equal in the sense of ability and competence. Without the capacity to identify and nurture the rare talents of the creative individual, organizations shrivel and lose their vitality.

The area of greatest sensitivity to the standards of equality is

[1] John Gardner, *Excellence* (New York: Harper & Row, 1961).

compensation. Organizations generate rewards in their transactions with the environment. They utilize resources such as money and manpower but the test of the efficiency of the organization is in its capacity to create a surplus of resources over and above those expended in the productive work of the organization. This surplus has to be distributed to the members, whether employees or stockholders. Some method of distribution must be achieved that is equitable and that sustains morale and the desire to continue to work hard. But equity in framing compensation plans cannot be confused with equality. Compensation plans try to take account of differences in inputs. Individuals with long service will usually receive more money than those with short service, even within the same occupation. The equity in this arrangement is to take account of the implications of an input like service and seniority. Interestingly enough, while managers recognize the need to reward service, it is also seen as a negative factor. Managers often complain that basing reward on seniority works against initiative.

The money rewards for work are not the only compensations subject to the sensitive reactions of equity and equality. Companies will often use elaborate procedures to assure an acceptable distribution of status rewards. Executives at the same level of the hierarchy are permitted an office with specified appurtenances. No one executive may deviate in size of office or decor, even though the needs for and uses of offices vary markedly with the type of job and the individual style of the executive.

The fear of inequality forces peculiar types of behavior patterns in organizations. Executives become sensitive to any implication that they enjoy working with one group member more than with another among their subordinates. This concern is reminiscent of the teasing and baiting directed to the "teacher's pet" of childhood days in school. The subtle rewards of recognition and esteem, warmth, and support must also, it would seem in the large-size organization, be distributed following the principle of equality. And yet, as every executive knows, it is inhuman to expect the same feelings and responses in relation to all subordinates. The differences in dispositions, personalities, what we as individuals like and dislike, command some sort of selective attention and response in our human relationships, *even* at work.

The main job of this chapter is to explore the psychology of equality, to understand its genesis and dynamics in the life experience of individuals. I will try to show that frequently the concern for equality, particularly on the part of the manager, is a reflection of his own personal sensitivities and conflicts and does not provide a realistic basis for executive action or organizational practice. I am particularly concerned here with misplaced emphasis on the compulsive practices addressed to the problem of equality in large organizations. This misplaced emphasis on procedure at the expense of judgment assures equal treatment, but fails to take account of the uniqueness of individuals and the differences in ability so vital to long-run effectiveness in work.

In particular, I want to explore the *feelings* connected with the quest for equality and to connect these emotional reactions to the individual's experiences in development. Then, I shall examine three main types of orientations to the paradox of equality in the face of obvious individual differences in ability. The first orientation is essentially the bureaucratic solution of emphasis on procedure. To a certain extent, all organizations must utilize procedures in establishing the conditions of work implied or expressed in the employment contract. But I am here concerned not with procedures as such, but with the orientations of executives who build their entire administrative approach around this depersonalized point of view.

The second orientation, found most commonly in organizations with a strong bureaucratic structure, is the solution by circumvention. Here particular executives recognize, on the one hand, the conditions leading to procedural emphasis in organizations as a means of securing equality, but use personally methods of circumventing these procedures to take account of individual differences. The technique of circumvention recognizes the form of impersonal procedures in assuring equality, but not its substance in terms of the desire to recognize special abilities.

A third orientation, one found less commonly in organizations but requiring more serious attention, is the positive approach to inequality. In this approach, the executive *begins with* individual differences—the fact that individuals are seldom alike in their abilities and interests. The positive approach to inequality, when coupled with equity and fairness, and the capacity to articulate the standards in back of this orientation, represents a different solution to the paradox of excellence and equality in modern organizations.

The Dynamics of Equality

The concern for equality begins with the fear that certain individuals will receive favored treatment or special consideration. This fear is connected with the potential problem of rivalry in organizations. If it does turn out that someone is given special consideration, then individuals may begin openly to compete with one another for rewards and exist as rivals for the limited gratifications in the organization.

The problem of rivalry is like a Pandora's box. Once opened, or experienced, it can loosen a whole set of conflicts for which organizations and individuals seem to establish only tenuous solutions. People would much prefer to suppress the basis of rivalry and even feign cooperation rather than to examine the consequences of differences. As a result the tendency develops to ignore individual differences at the expense of discouraging ability and initiative. Organizations avoid the conditions for rivalry even where the competition may result both in greater individual achievement and in organizational productivity.

One of the most sensitive problems of rivalry in organizations occurs during periods of management succession. There may be several key contenders for the number one position who, being naturally concerned about their chances for promotion, are unable to produce during the period of transition. The rivalry goes underground and may even be denied when, on the whole, it would be more effective for the individual and the organization if the key figures each developed and expressed his "platform" for the number one position. Of course, saving face and repairing injury to self-esteem is necessary, but no reason for avoiding differences and maintaining false illusions of equality and cohesion.

There is, in other words, an innate conservatism in the ideology of equality, cooperation, and harmony in human relationships. We can define this conservatism as a mechanism of avoidance. The underlying meaning is to suppress the condition of rivalry either because it appears too disruptive or because it generates uncomfortable feelings. The tendency therefore is to establish a balance in the relationships among men and to maintain this balance as a status quo. Any force seeking to upend or change the balance is resisted and countered. Yet we know that in the final analysis the balance shifts and the status quo dissolves either because of the force of events or the special catalytic effects of the individual, who lives outside the status quo, attacks it, and in the end leads the way to change.

The problem of explaining the dynamics of equality is essentially dual: (1) to explain the forces leading to the suppression of differences, or the artificial conditions of cooperation; (2) to explain the emergence of conflict, and the inequality implied in the condition of leadership where the individual lives outside of and in turn alters the existing balance in organizations. Both explanatory themes grow out of understanding the experience in the family during early development. It is during this period of life that the initial problem of rivalry and the threat of unequal treatment cuts most deeply. And we should not be surprised to see the parallel between the problem of rivalry in organizations and in the family. The family is, after all, the prototype of all organizations and becomes the primitive referent for the individual in his later work experience in organizations. This includes above all the manager whose own orientation to equality and the problem of rivalry can usually be traced to the mechanisms by which he dealt with similar issues in childhood in his relationships with siblings and parents.

Sibling Rivalry in the Family

The prototypical organization, as we have pointed out, is the family. The parents exist as the authority figures, the dispensers of reward and punishment. The siblings exist as the dependent figures who relate to one another in their common identification with the parents. Sigmund Freud outlined the main elements of group psychology around the configuration of the parental figure who succeeds in drawing into himself the emotional investments of subordinates.[2] Insofar as members of the group identify with him, they have a figure in common who acts as a cohesive force in the relations among the group members. Whatever divisive influences exist, these are suppressed or subordinated to the common interest in the attachment to the leader or parent figure.

But the basis of group cohesion and cooperation around the central figure, either leader or parent, is always uneasy. Cooperation is secondary in the emotional life of the individual and is preceded by the most intense feelings of hostility and rivalry in relation to siblings or any other object that appears to interfere with the primary attachment between child and parent.

The feelings that precede the cooperation based on common identifications spin out around the pervasive wish to attract and hold the parent, beginning with the mother and moving on to the father, as one's exclusive possession. There is an unconscious fantasy or wish that at one time in life the state of bliss of sole possession in fact existed. The reality in back of the fantasy, of course, is the unity between mother and infant.

The continuation of this fantasy proceeds along the following lines. This state of bliss, the representation of the Garden of Eden, would have persisted through eternity if it had not been for the appearance of the rival. The reality in back of the appearance of the rival is, of course, the birth of the younger child who displaces the older as the central recipient of gratifications.

[2] See his *Group Psychology and the Analysis of the Ego*, in *The Complete Psychological Works of Sigmund Freud*, Vol. XVIII, Standard Edition (London: Hogarth Press, 1955).

Clinical studies of the neuroses and of child development show that the experience of displacement and its effects on the fantasy of primacy is accompanied by the most intense feelings, including rage, and the near panic associated with helplessness. These emotional reactions to displacement are more uniform than we would suppose from commonsense observation. In the eyes of the adult, parents love the displaced child no less, but only devote more attention and care to the most dependent and helpless, namely, the newborn infant. But in the eyes of the displaced sibling, particularly when the ego is so fragile and incapable of understanding the nature of changes in the family, the injury and loss are severe. It is as though the world of the family consists of a finite amount of love and esteem available from parents. Any newcomer is seen as an interloper, an unwelcome intruder who commands a disproportionate share of the finite quantities of life-giving rewards. "The more who share the rewards," so the formula goes, "the less there is for me."

The quality and intensity of the emotions surrounding displacement are more nearly uniform than we may realize. But the outcome of the conflict generated by sibling rivalry varies depending upon many forces in the family constellation and within the individual himself. Sibling rivalry is handled differently if one is the oldest, the middle child, or the youngest in the family. For the oldest child the opportunity for dealing with the conflict by taking the role of parent surrogate in the relations with younger siblings leads to one sort of outcome. To the youngest child who may be the initial target for the hostility from siblings, sustained maternal protection usually leads to a somewhat different outcome. In the case of the middle child, the issue may be even more problematic. The resolutions of the oldest and the youngest may not be readily available, leading to a kind of withdrawal into fantasy whose potential may not be realized until the middle child succeeds in using fantasy for some sort of creative work.

Differences in the outcome of sibling rivalry are also related to the way parents behave in relation to children. Such factors as the capacity of the parents to tolerate and help channel the aggression generated in their children as a result of displacement are important. Usually, the way parents deal with the aggression in their children depends on their own resolutions of feelings of hostility. If the balance of emotional reactions in the parents is tenuous they will act to block and repress these reactions in the child. It is in this sense that history repeats itself. As one experiences the parent-child relationship, one tends to repeat the pattern with the roles reversed in later life.

The initial experience of rivalry then, occurs in the experience of displacement in the family, in the condition known as sibling rivalry. But a series of transformations occur in response to the conflicts aroused over the rivalrous feelings, which are usually quite intense. If one cannot achieve and maintain primacy in relation to the reward-giving parent, one then settles in deeply in the feeling that all should be treated alike. This response is the basic force toward the principle of equality and social justice. It impels the establishment of group relationships.

The thrust for equality stems not only from the reactions to the hostile feelings connected with displacement. It stems also from adopting and taking within oneself the basic attitudes of parents. Instead of hating the younger siblings one loves them following the example of the parents.

In one company, a key executive experienced intense feelings of anger and fear upon being criticized by others. These feelings, however, never found useful outlets, such as converting the anger into energetic discussion of the critic's point of view, including where necessary attack upon the other person's ideas. Instead, this man became silent and passive at the slightest show of criticism and would express agreement and positive feelings instead of the genuine anger that was evident even to the casual observer. The inability to deal with and use his own anger resulted from the fear of aggression seen in himself and in others and from the attempt to cope with the problem through turning the emotion into its opposite—instead of anger, show affection, and instead of criticism, show support. This pattern, incidentally, leads the person to a position of submissiveness and actually illustrates the masochism described in the last chapter.

The movement toward the principle of equality as a substitute for the position of the favored one is the basis of group formation. Identifications with the parents and their attitudes as the common ideal of the group are powerful forces sustaining cohesion. The maintenance of the cooperative feelings in group cohesion depends, however, on belief in either the myth or reality of equality: that each individual shares and shares alike. Yet we know that equality is constantly put to the test because of individual differences. The potential to create and contribute, particularly among adults in work organizations, is vastly different. The effects that occur when the myth of equality begins to break down or is sorely put to the test by the reality considerations of achievement include the outbreak of the earlier attitudes of hostility. These effects are amply demonstrated in the hostile attitudes directed toward the "ratebuster." It is described most clearly in the biblical story of Joseph and his brothers and it would be worth our while to re-examine this story in light of the problem of equality and rivalry in organizations.

The Story of Joseph and His Brothers

Joseph was the next to youngest son in the family of brothers. When their father, Jacob, presented him with a gift of a coat of many colors, this gift, singled out one brother for special treatment, and violated the tenet of equal treatment as a basis of group cohesion in the family. The brothers could hardly turn on the father who violated the tenet, but instead expressed their reawakened hatred toward the favored one. Joseph was later saved from the pit in which they cast him for revenge, and when he became a favored one to the Pharaoh, he helped his brothers in their time of need during the famine.

The moral we tend to draw from this biblical story is the virtue of forgiveness. One should not bear a grudge or live by the law of the talon: "an eye for an eye and a tooth for a tooth."

But the importance of the moral for social relationships should not mask the impelling quality of the condition of rivalry. It is always latent and subject to rekindling at the mere suggestion of favored treatment in violation of the principle of equality. This awareness of the latent effects of rivalry operates on many executives in their tenacious refusal to single out individuals for special treatment, no matter what special gifts of ability they bring to their work. This awareness also accounts for the problems encountered by the so-called "crown prince" in the organization, one who has been selected for succession to a post of leadership. The crown prince is vulnerable to attack from his "siblings" much as Joseph was in his relation to his brothers.

This vulnerability of the crown prince accounts for the not uncommon failure he experiences upon succeeding to the leadership position. As a target of attack, his subordinates who once were in the position of siblings may await his least error to fall upon him as vultures on a dying man. When the crown prince is destroyed the succession may be carried out more easily by a relatively anonymous figure who harbored ambitions but was aware of the pitfalls of being the crown prince and therefore remained in the background. In this connection we can cite the experiences of leadership succession in the Soviet Union following Stalin's death and Anthony Eden's succession following Churchill's retirement. In both cases, neither of the crown princes, or leader designates, could sustain his position. How much of the failure is attributed to the attacks from the siblings or the anxiety surrounding fantasy of such attacks is difficult to say. It is important, however, to recognize the vulnerability of the favored position and the reactions to the violation of the tenet of equality as a basis for cooperation among peers.

The Functions of Group Formations beyond the Family

The demand for equality in the eyes of the authority figure is the basis for group feeling and cooperation. This sense of the group is established initially in the family as a reaction formation to the hostility and sense of rivalry among siblings. Once the sense of the group becomes a part of the individual's deeply rooted attitudes, he is able to move out of the family context and establish similar group relationships at school and among playmates. The norm of equality becomes the foundation upon which these group relationships flourish and at the same time it becomes reinforced through continuing group experiences.

Jean Piaget, the Swiss Psychologist, has thrown considerable light on the social functions of the group of youngsters ranging in age from five or six to preadolescence.[3] Children learn more about cooperation and sharing through collaborative play activity. Piaget stresses the idea that this social learning proceeds rapidly because it occurs apart from the constraining presence of adult authority figures. The learning consists of an understanding of the function of rules in group activity. If the children play marbles, for example, they learn from the older and more experienced child how the game proceeds. This learning may occur merely through observation of the game or through direct participation. At any rate, the reward for learning the rules and observing them is heightened pleasure in the game and the exercise of new competences.

The importance to the child that the rules be observed is reflected in the negative, that is, when one of the youngsters breaks the rules. This violation of the standards of acceptable group conduct produces rage and usually results in outcasting from the group. This punishment is apt to be severe and acts to reinforce the conscience in the form of "the dread of the community."[4] The group experience of casting out a member who violates the code of conduct provokes guilt and anxiety in all members and not just in the object of the attack. The capacity of group punishments to provoke the reactions of conscience also serves to reinforce the strength of the norm of equality.

Besides learning something about rules and their value in cooperative activity, the youngster learns important distinctions about

[3] See his *The Moral Judgment of the Child* (New York: Harcourt Brace, 1932).

[4] See S. Freud, *Totem and Taboo*, Standard Edition, Vol. XIII.

the nature of justice. He learns, probably in connection with group activity, the foundation of retributive justice, or punishment. He makes the distinction between the intent and consequences of action and that punishment in a just manner should take into consideration the intent. This distinction is a part of our legal framework so that it is in fact a sophisticated social gain. But in addition to accepting the difference between intent and consequence the child still clings to the core notion of equality. Punishment should be meted out equally as a condition of justice; if there is the slightest indication of favored treatment in punishment and discipline, the individuals in the group react with anger.

The social and moral gains of the group experiences before adolescence serve valuable ends in securing the conditions of cooperation. The kindred feelings dampen the aggression that still lurks below the surface in the siblinglike atmosphere of the group. The children work and play together and discharge aggression through the common activity rather than through rivalry.

While recognizing the social significance of equality as it becomes firmly established during the early school years, we must also remind ourselves of the unsolved problem of individuality. Some educators and social scientists seem to fix their concern with development at the point where the social awareness of the person may be at its peak during the school years. They almost idealize and perpetuate the model of the peer group as the solution for human problems in organization and society.

The point that I want to stress is that while valuable, these social lessons answer only half the problem of how the person shall live and work in a complex society. The other half of the problem turns around the issue of individuality and creativity. It also turns around the question of altering the status quo since the lessons of group experiences are mainly conservative in character: how to maintain that which exists in human affairs.

If large-scale organizations become dominantly conservative in fostering the rules of equality without establishing the values of individuality, then we can expect to find a persistent diminution of vigor and initiative.

Fortunately, development does not stop with the experience of the play group of preadolescence. Equality and individuality are tested further in the group experiences of adolescence.

Group Behavior during Adolescence

The paradoxical qualities of individuality and equality can be seen most clearly in the group patterns of adolescence. We are most aware of the fact that the adolescent strives to be different and unconventional. The bizarre appearance of the "beatnik," the rapid innovations in dance and play, all testify to the rejection of the conventional modes of life. Yet while striving to be different, the adolescent is painfully conformist in his relations with peers. To be out of style, to use expressions and dress that were "in" six months ago, but that are "out" now is a humiliating experience for the adolescent.

The conventions that are criticized belong to the world of the adults—mainly the parents. The standards of conformity belong to the special world of the adolescent. To reject one set of standards only to live slavishly by another expresses the singularly difficult task of adolescence: to free the individual from the family as a step toward accepting the responsibilities of independence and adulthood.

The group patterns of adolescence, curiously, provide opportunities for going beyond the solution of equality rooted in the family. The adolescent culture demands equal treatment at the hands of authority figures, but the group seen from the inside differentiates members. The adolescent group is a stratified structure; individuals assume leadership, are admired for what they can do; or, conversely, are relegated to the position of follower and even devalued in the eyes of their peers.

This stratification and practice in leadership holds true whether in the gang of delinquents or the highly creative world of the student as artist, musician, poet, or scientist. William Foote

Whyte provided one of the most sensitive studies of the group formations of adolescence and in it described the nature of stratification and the leader-follower relationship.[5]

The Nortons were a typical street-corner gang held together by their leader, Doc. Whyte studied the Nortons by participating in their life so that he presents us with a picture drawn from the "inside" view. Statuses in the gang were allocated according to the capacity of the group members to generate rewarding activities for the group. This capacity in turn depended on the individual's position in the wider hierarchy of the community, particularly in relation to its political organization. Doc was most influential outside the group and consequently within the group. But this outside influence was not the whole story. He was admired as a person by his group members and performed well in those activities valued by the group, including bowling and other social activities.

The group structure took the form of the pyramid with Doc at the top. The level below him consisted of his lieutenants, most of whom were leaders of subgroups. Communication within the group followed the channels of the subgroups up to the lieutenants and from them to Doc. The group generally was immobilized unless Doc was present and approved its activities. The group was democratic to the extent that initiation of ideas and activities could come from below, but their fruition into a group effort depended on the approval of the leader.

Whyte's study showed that the group members invested strong emotional meaning in the existence and perpetuation of their hierarchy. Members were able to resist successfully efforts to alter the statuses of members through a variety of subtle group controls. From the standpoint of individuals in the group, the life in it represented anything but the theme of equality in social relationships. But its inequality, in the form of differences in status within the group emerged as a product of group relationships. It was not imposed from without. If the group had formed

[5] See his study, *Street Corner Society* (Chicago: University of Chicago Press, 1943).

around an external authority figure the theme of equality would probably have been quite strong. This group, like most adolescent groups, was separated from outside authority and its social behavior a spontaneous product of issues facing the members.

The group experience of adolescence in many ways may prepare its members for individuality by giving them experience in the formation of a leadership structure. The critical issue of adolescence, however, is whether the individuals and the group can resolve and sustain a position with respect to equality and authority beyond the limits of the autonomous group. If the groups can sustain leadership only in antagonism to the wider authority structure of society, then there would seem to be little basis for resolving the dilemmas inherent in the earlier rigid adherence to ideals of equality. Those who succeed in achieving leadership in the adolescent group cannot realize individuality if the conditions of leadership are not of a kind valued in the society at large. The leadership exists as a negative expression, and this is exemplified best in the delinquent gang that supports collectively impulsive behavior.

Fixations in Group Behavior

Many adults during their careers never succeed in going beyond the developmental gains of the school and adolescent years. The failure is in the limited sense of independence. Their performance as adults represents a fixation in development in which their psychological reactions are imbedded in their identifications with groups. This fixation, while establishing a balance for the individual in his social relationships, works against excellence in performance and creativity. The job of the adult is to liberate himself from group psychology and to achieve individual identity with responsibility.

For the adult, the thrust toward equality reappears as strongly as it existed in the family and the peer group of the school years. Coupled with equality is the preference for group interaction as the setting for work as compared with either individual effort or the relationship of superior and subordinate, or colleagues.

The desire for equality leads to a generally conservative attitude and to a preference for harmony and cooperation as the media of work rather than vigorous effort and differences. This preference in work styles results in a dampening of energy and the fostering of passivity. Its opposite, activity, forces a confrontation with the unreality of much of the ritual of equality.

While studying adult group behavior, I have often been struck with the appearance of ritual designed to mask over the bases of differentiation among members. The rituals in effect reassert the demand for equality and the reduction of the capacity of one member to influence others. They act as a force to counter the potential rivalry among members. In one study of an advertising agency, for example, the account group meetings could not begin without joking and the play-out of a fining ritual. Members would fine one another for coming in late or saying something critical of another person. Usually the persons fined most frequently, or the butt of the joking, were figures who had relatively high status in the group and whose job required them to direct activity.

The presence of joking behavior and other ritual is seemingly harmless, but it is not insignificant. In my studies of group behavior I have found consistently that this behavior leads the way to many of the important tensions in work and human relationships in organizations. Invariably the tensions are rooted in the rivalrous feelings generated in the course of work. When the rivalries. come out into the open, the ritualistic behavior disappears.

Another indication of this fixation is the presence of strong pressures to conform. Members punish the individual who deviates from the rigid standards of the group whether or not the deviation is realistic and potentially productive. Studies of conformity and deviation in groups show just how group pressures work.[6] The individual who deviates becomes the center of inter-

[6] See Stanley Schachter, "Deviation, Rejection and Communication," *Group Dynamics*, Cartwright and Zander, eds. (Evanston: Row, Peterson, 1956).

action. Members address themselves to him in an effort to force him to conform. If they succeed, he moves back into the usual patterns of the group. If the pressures fail to restore conformity, then the individual is isolated from the group. The individual is then faced with the problem of sustaining his position but without support. This isolation puts the individual to a severe test.

The extent of the power of group pressures is reflected in a now classic study of conformity in groups conducted by the social psychologist, Solomon Asch.[7] In a series of experiments he found that as many as a third of the population in his experiments would distort reality in the interests of maintaining a conformist position. Interestingly enough the individuals who would weigh their reactions according to their sense of reality and away from the pressures of the group were those who seemed strongly motivated by the need to achieve.

Many, perhaps the majority, of adults in pursuing their career remain fixated at the level of group membership. The question remains: Why do these forms persist and why is the pressure for equality and sameness in human relationships so pervasive among adults? The answer to this question brings us back to the problem of rivalry and the work of reaction formation in maintaining a balanced economy of forces in the inner life of the individual. Presumably reaction formation, or the reversal of attitude, is not the only solution to the problem of aggression and rivalry in human relationships. As individuals and organizations work toward other solutions, perhaps the way may be found to liberate individual creativity and excellence.

Defending against Rivalry

I indicated earlier in this chapter that the roots of the problem of rivalry are to be found in the experience in the family, particularly in the relations among siblings. The sequence begins with the fantasy of maintaining the primary position of being the cen-

[7] S. E. Asch, *Social Psychology* (Englewood Cliffs, N. J.: Prentice-Hall, 1952).

tral figure in the life-giving relationship with the mother. This fantasy is interrupted rudely by the birth of a younger sibling. This displacement also resonates against the feelings of rivalry in the Oedipus complex discussed in the preceding chapter. The rivalry is accompanied by the most intense hostile-aggressive feelings that generate conflict within the individual over the fear of complete loss of love and protection from parents.

Investigation of this early condition of rivalry on the part of the adult usually leads to a reaction something like this: that the feeling of rivalry, of hate and hostility in the relationships among siblings is *abnormal*. The adult usually maintains the position that love and consideration among siblings is the *normal* condition. Persons who see sibling relationships in this fashion are themselves affected by the work of reaction formation—the turning of hatred into love as a defense against anxiety. There is nothing abnormal about rivalry. In fact, it becomes a condition of development and a potential for growth, because just how the individual deals with the conflict establishes the pattern for later fixation into group psychology or for individuation.

The work of reaction formation converts the hostile and rivalrous feeling into love and consideration, following the attitudes of the parents. By and large, the work of reaction formation serves as a useful defense against anxiety and as a force toward the establishment of altruistic attitudes and a sense of the community. But reaction formation may occur too abruptly and rigidly. It may impose restrictive patterns of behavior and generate a very low tolerance for aggression and differences. This condition accompanies passivity and inhibition in work and human relationships. The person experiences himself only in the reflections he gets back from other people. He can tolerate and seeks mainly the reflection that he is "a good guy." Any other reflection tends to reawaken the aggression and hostility that is inevitably there and unchanneled in the form of productive performance.

The fact that the experience of sibling rivalry and the accompanying solution through reaction formation is universal leads to the perpetuation of the myth of equality in group relationships. Individuals have a way of intersecting one another in their common life problems. They will form collective means for sustaining their own position of defense, for avoiding the problems so tenuously bypassed in the course of development. In this way, groups and organizations reflect the way individuals deal with anxiety and serve as a defensive structure of the community much the same way the towns in medieval times grew up around a fortress designed to ward off the enemy from without. In this case, the "enemy" really exists within the individual. The myth of equality and the problem of rivalry is in reality a condition of existence of the person. How he chooses to use this condition is prophetic for the type of individual he becomes. How an organization represents this condition in the collective relations among its members goes a long way toward sustaining the inadequate choices so frequently observed in the compulsiveness of the adults in their careers.

ORGANIZATIONAL SOLUTIONS OF THE PROBLEM OF RIVALRY

The concept of an organizational solution for the problem of rivalry is in many ways a contradiction. I do not believe realistically there is a solution which will remain intact for any length of time. We are dealing with a problem that can be solved, if at all, only by the individual. And the way the individual resolves the dilemma varies from one person to the next and even shifts for him depending on his progress in development. Organizational solutions have a way of becoming unstuck, suggesting that we are dealing with something resembling a dialectic. Once a solution is established, a set of counteracting forces begins to shake it loose until a new solution has to emerge. This can be seen easily in the oscillations in organizations between practices of centralization and decentralization, between promoting respect for status and rituals of equality. The swings may be measured in years or decades. In some cases they may be best measured in centuries as in the case of the Roman Catholic Church whose internal struggles over the relative positions of the Pope and his bishops, of the Curia and the diocese reflect the dramatic quality and the never-ending struggle over the problem of rivalry in human relationships.

I cannot hope to treat the question of organizational solutions in exhaustive fashion. There are, however, three general types of solutions worth considering here. The first is toward bureaucracy and the condition of distributive justice; the second is the solution by circumvention; and the third, a problematic solution, is the positive approach to rivalry and *inequality*. Let us consider each of these solutions in turn.

Distributive Justice and the Bureaucratic Solution

Max Weber, the German sociologist, is famous for his descriptions of a bureaucratic organization.[8] He presented his views of bureaucracy as a type of organization stressing rational-legal procedures in administration. Administrators in bureaucratic organizations function *sine ire et studio*, without emotionally coloring their behavior. The establishment of power relations in bureaucracy as well as methods of compensation, promotion, and discipline depends on rules and procedures, usually written. Codification is important in the ideal type of bureaucracy so that the rules by which relationships are governed are clearly visible and may be applied equally to all.

The success of the bureaucratic, or legal-procedural, approach to organization depends on the willingness of men to invest their confidence in the administration. Clearly, confidence does not develop merely on the orderliness by which rules are administered. Organizations depend for success on the performance of services that are valued in the environment. They serve clients who are not interested in how orderly the organization is managed, but rather on a competitive basis, how valuable the products are. General Motors indeed may have the finest set of

[8] See his *Theory of Social and Economic Organization*, trans. A. M. Henderson and Talcott Parsons (Glencoe, Ill.: Free Press, 1947).

rules and procedures covering all its employees equally. The success of General Motors and the long-run commitment of its employees depend on its competitive position in producing and selling automobiles.

If organizations existed as closed systems, that is, without any transactions with their environment, then it would be possible for the bureaucratic model to function. Because organizations are open systems the emphasis of activity is always directed outward. Internal administration is therefore a means and not the end in itself.

Sociologists have long directed criticism at the bureaucratic model because its officials tend to "displace" goals. Bureaucratic managers tend to give priority to the means of administration and not to its purposes. The means of administration like job evaluation plans, organization charts, and procedures and rules are by themselves not productive. If these means become the ends of organization as they are likely to become in the hands of unimaginative people who thrive in bureaucracies, then organizational effectiveness may be sorely damaged. In the long run as the effectiveness of an organization diminishes, its members lose confidence in it and finally undermine the very premises upon which the legal-procedural concept depends in organization management.

Bureaucracy is designed principally to assure equality in the treatment of employees and to suppress rivalry. One of the principles upon which bureaucratic procedure depends in maintaining equality is *distributive justice*. All individuals are treated alike, in this ideal type, because they are subject to the same rules. The rule of reward and compensation, most fundamental to the motivation of employees, is founded on the notion that rewards are distributed in proportion to the individual's inputs. The rule of proportionality, stated in Aristotle's *Nichomachean Ethics* as the principle of distributive justice, maintains equality while permitting differentiation in compensation.

Individuals receive different amounts of pay and benefits, but these are distributed in proportion to differences in skill, responsibility, the training required to man the job, and other factors representing the individual's social investments in his job. In fact, we recognize the rule of proportionality in the structure of most job evaluation plans, including the plan set forth by Elliot Jacques that is supposed to permit all employees, from president to janitor, to live within the same wage structure.[9] Criticisms of job evaluation plans in the past have centered mainly on adaptability to hourly jobs and not to executive, creative, and abstract types of work. According to Jacques this limitation can be overcome by building job evaluation plans according to the principle of time span of the work as an evaluative factor. Closer scrutiny of Jacques' plan or any other for that matter shows that salary differentials cannot be supported *logically* on the basis of the rule of distributive justice. Proportionality will not explain the vast salary differentials in American industry, including stock option plans, retirement programs, and other benefits.

The basic reason why proportionality applies only within the strata of organizations and not between them (like the comparison of hourly and salaried employees) is the competitive pressure for talented people. Corporate executives recognize in the final analysis that creative individuals are hard to come by and command rewards that cannot be justified on the rational rule of proportionality but rather on the more primitive principle of the free market in competing for talent.

In other words, the bureaucratic solution to the problem of rivalry, of stressing procedures to assure equality in treatment, by and large does not work except within rather narrow divisions of the hierarchy. It is on the whole a good thing that the rule of the market place still functions. Without it, the respect for talent would diminish and the vitality of organizations would disappear.

There is another indication of the failure of the bureaucratic solution to the problem of rivalry. It is commonplace to observe that bureaucratic organizations tend to foster a form of unpro-

[9] See his book, *Equitable Payment* (London: Heinemann, 1961).

ductive rivalry called empire building. Executives compete with one another in establishing power centers under their command through manipulation of procedures. One executive, for example, proposes a new procedure designed to regulate and control internal relations; and to implement this new technique, he needs a staff. Then as described in Parkinson's law, staffs tend to create work to fill the time, or for which they are capable. This in turn generates new demands for internal procedures and coordinating devices like committees. As staff increases and committee memberships proliferate a hidden status system emerges. Executives begin to vie with one another in suggesting new procedures for internal regulation, designed to assure equality, only in the end to see a vicious type of rivalry dominate, vicious in the sense that this bureaucratic rivalry is not addressed to the productive purposes of the organization and is therefore wasteful of human resources.

Reliance on the bureaucratic solution tends to occur during periods marked by relative harmony and balance in the relationship between an organization and its environment. When competitive pressures from other organizations lessen, or the challenges to the organization are at a minimum, orientation tends to be turned inward, and the proceduralists hold sway. But such periods of harmony are relatively short lived. With the appearance of crisis, of challenge from outside the organization, emphasis on bureaucratic procedure and its rigid adherence to equality diminishes. It is usually during crises that another solution is tried, built on the principle of circumvention.

The Solution of Circumvention

Crises call forth the best work man is capable of producing. Unfortunately crises are thrust upon us in the form of war, of social and economic disaster, and usually reflect the failings of human relationships. But the irony of the situation should not mislead us into believing that man works best under conditions of quiescence.

We wonder, for example, if the advances in science and education beginning in the late 1950s could have occurred apart from the appearance of the Russian sputnik. The temper of the times was the yearning for peace and quiet. President Eisenhower reflected this yearning in his style of administration which essentially was bureaucratic. The period saw few innovations and ideas that had a forward thrust in terms of solving world and domestic problems. Along came sputnik, which acted as a blow to American pride. This blow led to searching re-examination and rapid innovation in our scientific enterprise and our educational system.

The impelling force of crisis leads to rapid innovation in organizations. The premium is placed on ideas and imagination rather than on procedure and the tired solutions imbedded in administrative techniques. The issue is no longer one of maintaining balance and equality, but of locating and bringing to the fore the idea men with the courage and tenacity to see their ideas through.

While fostering innovation, leaders during crises seem also to be wary of destroying the bureaucratic structure. They therefore maintain the structure, on the one hand, but seek for innovation, on the other, through circumvention. The rise during the Second World War of new agencies in government permitted the attraction of brilliant executives who could innovate outside the bureaucratic agencies. The use of special assistants without title or portfolio is another example of the solution by circumvention. The special assistant's power stems from his proximity to the chief executive and his personal competence. It does not stem from his investment in a hierarchy. The statement of Clemenceau that "war is too important to leave to the generals," reflects the philosophy of bypassing the bureaucracy during times of crisis.

Circumvention creates a high degree of inequality in power and reward. Not only are special considerations used in the course of circumvention, but it patently ignores the rules designed to maintain equality in relationships. The justification, of course, is the crisis. It is important to recognize, however, that circumvention works best if it does not frontally attack the bureaucracy and the theme of equality. True circumvention operates on the principle of coexistence of the new and the traditional. But by sheer dint of ability and imagination, the innovative generally makes the greatest impact toward the solution of the crisis.

The reason circumvention avoids frontal attack on the bureaucracy is the desire to keep resistance to a minimum. During Franklin D. Roosevelt's administration, he encountered the greatest resistance to change and failure when he launched a frontal attack on the Supreme Court during the famous "packing" episode. Resistance was mobilized and concentrated to a degree he could not cope with.

The solution of circumvention uses the art of ambiguity and it fosters rivalry. The head of a staff group in a headquarters office and the line executive do compete for influence, because there is no way through procedural definition to establish and contain the areas of influence. The circumventor uses this ambiguity expecting the rivalry generated to produce better solutions than highly cooperative and coordinated activity.

Where bureaucracy fosters orderliness, equality, and proportionality, circumvention fosters ambiguity, competitiveness, and shifting rewards. Bureaucracy is oriented inward, toward maintaining harmony and balance. Circumvention is oriented outward toward the solution of problems usually of crisis proportions. The principle of circumvention works best when it does not attack frontally the bureaucratic structure and the ideology of equality. Its main failing is in its inability to sustain itself. Once crises pass, the yearning for quiescence results in a restoration of bureaucratic primacy. This fact is reflected in the work of management succession. The characteristics of the successor reflect the tenor of the demands on the organization.

The oscillation between equality and rivalry, between bureaucratic and circumventive styles of management, raises questions about the possibility of other solutions of excellence and equality. Other solutions remain speculative, largely because of the doubt whether there is realistically an organizational solution to a human dialectic like rivalry and equality. But it would be worthwhile to explore, if only speculatively, the nature of a positive approach to rivalry and inequality as conditions fostering excellence and achievement.

A Positive Approach to Rivalry and Inequality

Suppose we adopt a premise usually foreign to traditional thought about organization and human relations. The premise is that rivalry and inequality by themselves are not bad (psychologically or morally). They reflect the upsurge of aggressive energy which is part of the human endowment. Without aggression there would be no control and survival in an environment which is not especially congenial to human existence. Following this premise, the main question is how aggression and the rivalry that goes with it are to be channeled and used. There are, presumably, relatively effective and ineffective, moral and immoral forms of using aggression.

The bureaucratic approach, particularly as it becomes overlaid with many ideas from human relations practitioners, adopts the opposite premise. It seeks through procedural solutions to foster equality and harmony with the consequence that aggression is blocked and turned inward, fostering the timid and passive personality.

The solution by circumvention fails mainly in its inability to anticipate crises and needs. It tends to emerge in reaction to dangerous situations already thrust upon us. A new solution would foster a kind of thought and performance that is able to anticipate problems. In addition it is haphazard in the development of talent. Circumvention uses talent that already exists but makes no special contribution toward developing excellence in individuals.

An approach that begins with the value of rivalry and inequality seeks appropriate channels for their expression. The question of selecting channels begins with the need to define useful goals toward which rivalry can be used as an instrument of action. If the goals meet the test of human purposes, then the aggression with which they are pursued is humanized. The rivalry, competition, and resulting inequality in evaluation are seen in the perspective of achieving human ends. The aggression is not directed at individuals as in warfare, but at nature and in the pursuit of excellence and competence.

The positive approach to rivalry also seeks for consensus on the importance of excellence. Organizations must therefore be willing to single out and differentiate individuals according to their varying competence. While individuals may try equally hard to contribute, the value of their performance is not measured by effort, but rather by results. This approach to compensation, reward, and promotion is seemingly rigorous, but it is neither unjust nor depersonalized. It especially avoids the injustice of judging a man by who he is and his personal characteristics rather than by his contribution.

I am identifying an organizational philosophy rather than a set of procedures for this positive approach to inequality. It depends foremost on the leadership of an organization, on the ability of leaders to establish and communicate goals and standards that can excite the imagination of participants. The degree of confidence leaders have in this philosophy and the goals that emerge from it communicates itself to others and acts to inspire the work of the individual. In this way, this approach begins with the value of individual effort rather than the group per se. Whether individuals work best alone or in collaborative settings is not relevant because the conditions of work will vary depending on the tasks and the persons involved. I believe that fostering the ideals of group effort and devaluing the work of the individual has a negative effect.

In general, leaders of organizations would do well to minimize their prescriptions on style of work and leave this to the outcomes of expression of individual differences. The emphasis is on the goals and their articulation, along with the prizing of high standards of performance. Under these conditions, there will appear readily differences among individuals. But these differences will assert ideals that can be held in common and valued as the best expression of how man can use his abilities and the energies at his disposal.

BEYOND EQUALITY AND RIVALRY

The substitution of the ideals of performance and excellence in the end can dissolve for the individual the tensions of equality and rivalry. These tensions, as I have tried to demonstrate, are part and parcel of the developmental process. As such, the problem of rivalry and the attempted solution through equality represent transitions in development. It is true that if the individual does not master the rivalrous issue, or becomes fixated at the level of equality as a basis of group psychology, there is a failure in achieving the strengths of individuality.

Rivalry and equality are developmental crises for the individual. Organizations cannot solve the problem for him. But organizations can foster the ideals that make the developmental gains worth pursuing. It is here that leadership in business, education, and public affairs has yet to make a lasting contribution.

6 / *Discontinuities in Status and Self-Esteem*

An individual's sense of self-esteem is a product mainly of having achieved gratifications at appropriate periods in the life cycle followed by the capacity to move on in facing new challenges in development. Failure in gratification and the inability to renounce satisfactions no longer appropriate for the particular period in life reflect and grow out of depletions in self-worth.

Because individuals cannot live isolated existences and are relatively dependent upon persons and the environment, particularly during the early stages of development, the evaluation of self is frequently bound into the quality of the individual's transactions with his environment. The basic sense of trust, for example, reflects the person's orientation toward the environment. For the individual who has secured appropriate gratifications and has been able to progress in development, the sense of trust is expressed in a realistic view of the world in which gratification is possible and persons exist as objects to whom one may relate in satisfactory ways consistent with the type of relationship involved. The sense of distrust is often expressed around a basic view of a malevolent world. In the extreme, this sense of malevolence in the environment is a projection of the individual's own hostilities and destructive wishes toward figures in his past. In either case the person secures some type of feedback from his environment. In the case of trust and self-worth, the environment seems to provide confirmations of the individual's existence as a person and in his performance of roles at work, in the family, and the community; in the case of distrust, the feedback often reflects discontinuity in identity.

In organizations and occupations of various kinds symptoms of discontinuity between a person's status, on the one hand, and his sense of identity are often seen. This discontinuity seems bound into the conflicting messages which an individual receives from his environment, or in messages that while consistent in themselves fail to agree with the individual's own expectations.

Before generalizing about the types of discontinuities and their manifestations, it would be valuable to examine a case study. This case illustrates the sort of tensions existing within the individual that are closely related to the lack of confirmation in the interchange between person and environment.

Inconsistency in Expectation and Reality: The Case of Richard Carleton

Richard Carleton, aged fifty-seven, worked in a machining and assembly department selected for intensive study by a group of social scientists.[1] As a routine step in the research, I interviewed Carleton off the job and in the course of talks and observations over a seven-month period, I learned a great deal about his present and past life situation. Carleton was a markedly disturbed individual who found very little enjoyment and satisfaction in his activities in and out of work. He was hypochondriacal and under a doctor's constant care. Among his basic complaints was a sense of shame and disgust at himself, and the surroundings of work and living. He felt estranged from his social environment and

[1] For a report on this research, see A. Zaleznik, C. R. Christensen, and F. J. Roethlisberger, in collaboration with G. C. Homans, *The Motivation, Productivity and Satisfaction of Workers: A Prediction Study* (Cambridge: Division of Research, Harvard University Graduate School of Business Administration, 1958). See also A. Zaleznik and D. Moment, *The Dynamics of Interpersonal Behavior* (New York: John Wiley and Sons, 1964).

constantly criticized himself, suggesting that his expectations and potential identity were at variance with his reality. Much of the emotional reactions he experienced and expressed reflected a deep bitterness and disgust, qualities that stand in sharp contrast to the feelings of self-worth.

Carleton's story is of interest here because it illustrates one type of conflict between an individual's identity and reality, common in our highly mobile and changing society. This conflict centers around the state that sociologists call downward mobility —the case where the individual's social class as an adult is below that of his parents or the class to which his social conditioning had been oriented. Another type of conflict between identity and reality is, of course, upward mobility. In this case, the individual has many more material advantages than earlier in life, yet self-esteem is frequently tenuous. Whereas, in the case of downward mobility, as I shall show shortly in returning to Richard Carleton, the depletion in self-worth is experienced as shame and disgust; in the case of upward mobility, the emotions of anxiety and guilt tend to color the individual's subjective experience.

Taking upward and downward mobility as extreme instances of disparity between the individual's expectation and reality we can recognize other disparities that occur in particular positions in work organizations. In the total life situation of the person these disparities are less pervasive than mobility problems, yet they frequently produce the same emotional qualities in the experience of the individual.

The positions most vulnerable in this respect are those that operate at the boundaries of groups and organizations. The most widely reported boundary position fraught with potential disparities between expectation and reality is the job of the foreman. He has been characterized as "the man in the middle," the "master and victim of double talk," and "the marginal man" in the management of organizations. These terms seek to describe the problems facing the individual whose status is in doubt and consequently one whose confirmation of identity from his social reality is likewise in doubt.

But the problem of the boundary positions are not restricted to the lower-level supervisor. In this chapter, I shall delineate some of the positions in organizations that contain to a peculiar degree the problem of balancing or integrating disparities in status. For the moment, however, I would like to return to Richard Carleton who provides a basic illustration of the issue.

In introducing Richard Carleton I described the key symptoms he presented in interviews but merely touched on the facts about his present situation and past history. In his own words, Carleton said about his present life situation:

> With me it's like everyone else. There are no two people alike. No two peas in a pod. Maybe some people do things because of their own liking or because of things they can't control. With me, my whole reason for being here is because of things I can't control. I'm an individual doing things I shouldn't be doing. All of my life I've been doing things I shouldn't be doing.
>
> Now I am not in good health. My stomach is kicking up and I can't start out afresh. At night I go home and fall into a chair just so I can get enough strength to come in the next day. I force myself to like this job, but the job doesn't like me.

Carleton worked as an unskilled machinist. His work, along with most jobs in the department, was repetitive and required very little training to master. Carleton had this to say about the content of work in the department:

> There's no job here that I'd prefer, none whatsoever. The only job that's available for me is Joe's [the group leader], but I couldn't handle it. I just couldn't handle it. I can run a lathe all day as far as operating it goes, but I can't tear it down and then set it up and then I can't grind.

Carleton had no aspirations for other jobs in the department because he felt he had little skill and aptitude for the work. He said, "I'm not a mechanical man." In many ways, he was overconscientious in his work, approaching his job with obsessive deliberation. As a result, Carleton produced at low rates and came to the attention of the supervisor. This added considerably to his insecurity, and he said:

They've got me on edge on this job all the time. I try to give them what they want. I sit at the bench when the bell rings and I give them what they want, and I don't know how the others do it. I don't know how they turn their count in unless they lie. I'm just too tired.

The tension Carleton experienced in his work performance resulted in a vicious circle: the more the job got him down, the more fatigued he felt and less able to perform. As his perform-ance failed to meet job standards, Carleton had to face his super-visor, and this added to the insecurity and tension.

The work content, however, was only one among several fea-tures of his job that Carleton found frustrating. Most of the workers in the department were city born and bred and of Irish-Catholic background. Carleton came from a rural middle-class background and was a "Yankee" Protestant. He said:

You know we have an Irish city here. I guess eight out of ten people are Irish. There are only half a dozen Protestants here and I don't think there are even a half a dozen Jewish people. We have to stick together against the Romans. It's a ticklish subject to talk about. I try to be tolerant and I pray to God I can be tolerant but sometimes it's hard. Why their moral laws are of no significance compared to us. We had a Catholic priest at our church. He believed anything was right as long as deep down in your heart you want to do right. Next door to me there is a hall. They have weddings there. You should see all the whiskey they bring in and the drinking that goes on. We think our weddings are more serious and sacred. These other people I'm talking about, they're always going to the men's room. How they are able to do a day's work when they are always going to the men's room I'll never figure out. All they do is stand around and gab, and they are late, and they are always sitting around playing cards and gambling. They are not supposed to do it, but there's a central clique of fellows around here and all they do is gamble. They'll beat us to go to the church all right, but once out they don't give it a thought. They don't think about it at all until next week.

Carleton's sense of superiority over the Irish-Catholics in his department was based on his clinging to an earlier identity of a son of reasonably well-to-do professional parents. The loss of this identity, which I will discuss shortly, produced anger that he vented against his coworkers. Another target of his aggression was the women who worked in the department. The fact that women could do the same work he did, and in many cases better, presented to Carleton a disparaging comparison that he subsequently turned against the women. He felt that women, especially the married ones, should not be in the department doing "men's work." Despite a basically antiunion attitude on his part, Carleton felt the only remedy for the problem of the women at work was for the union to vote them out.

Carleton's hostile attitude toward his coworkers resulted in his isolation from whatever social interchange the department could offer an older worker. This isolation extended itself to his life outside the plant. Carleton was married, but had no children or other close family ties. Besides work, his main activity was the church choir. He felt he had musical talent and he used it in choir work. This activity, however, provided only limited satisfaction since he felt constantly tired and could not enjoy the rehearsals. He also resented the choir conductor who was paid for her work while he and his wife volunteered. In summarizing his present situation and attitudes, Carleton said:

I live in a triangle—here, church, and in the chair at home. . . . My wife never could have children. The only child I have is a four-legged mongrel dog. . . . I think my wife and I have only four people we can call our friends. In the old days when I ran the business, we had lots of friends. . . . I used to have my own business and then I supervised other people. I was good at that. The way I feel mentally I can't do anything. Whenever I get ready to turn over a new leaf I get physically exhausted. I just go home and rest and wake up in the morning totally exhausted. You know it's nerves, of course.

I'm 57 and my wife is 60 years old. We're not kids and we can't do things any more, not without our health. . . . If I had my health, I would be doing something about this. I would go into the musical game. My wife and I were both in it. We both loved it and wished we didn't have to leave it, but the depression wiped us out overnight. We had our own business. . . . it took us just like that. We haven't been off our street since 1932. No vacations, no trips, or anything. We just sit at home.

The good Lord meant me to be an outdoor man. I would give

anything if I could get away from it and into some quiet town, but what few friends we have are still here and my wife wouldn't want to go. Age has just got me licked.

Carleton's sense of despair and helplessness reflected a depletion in self-esteem and ego strength. The disparity between what he was supposed to amount to in life and his actual situation resulted in shame and disgust. And reality provided him with many opportunities to continue to make disparaging comparisons between this ideal self and the actual self, and between the ideal social and work situation and the actual one in which he found himself.

The note of helplessness and dependency running throughout Carleton's evaluations of himself went back a long way in his history. As indicated earlier, he was born in a middle-class family with adequate means. His father had been a professional man as had his father's father before him. Carleton never knew his father, who died when the boy was three years old. The lack of a strong masculine figure with whom to identify was a serious deprivation. His early life had been dominated by his mother, who went to work to support her family. Carleton felt she had been very strict and demanding, especially with respect to orderliness and cleanliness. There was an absence in his description of his early childhood of the experiences that build a strong ego and a sense of self-esteem.

It is interesting to note that he married a woman older than himself and upon whom he shifted his dependency needs. His wife, through her family, provided him with a business that later failed. From all indications, his wife ran the household and controlled all the expenditures. His sphere of decision and independence was highly restricted.

In presenting this case history, I have tried to show how a discontinuity between an individual's expectations of what he was supposed to become in life and his actual situation serves as a feeding ground for other serious neurotic disturbances. The cause of the neurosis is to be found in the history and development of the individual. Yet the basis of the complaints in the present situation is revealing of some of the components of the sense of self-esteem as it functions in the life of the adult with occupational responsibilities.

The components of the sense of self-esteem notable in their absence in Carleton's case include a work activity related to the individual's competences; an identification with individuals in the immediate social environment, including some sharing of interests and aspirations; a balance in the relations of intimacy between dependence and independence, or a reasonable distribution between giving and getting in human relationships; a reasonable sense of control over events and outcomes, where one feels neither omnipotent nor subject to arbitrary and malevolent forces. These components serve to enhance the individual's sense of self-worth and as such are closely interrelated. The person cannot easily enter into mutual relations with others with whom he has great difficulty in identifying. And, in the absence of objects with whom to communicate, the sense of perspective about the control of events is frequently difficult to manage.

To illustrate the way consistency between expectations and social reality helps to secure the satisfactions necessary to the maintenance of the sense of self-worth, consider a second case that stands in sharp contrast to Richard Carleton's situation. Interestingly enough, the material is drawn from the same factory and work department as Richard Carleton's. This second case, therefore, emphasizes the differences in outcomes possible when there is consistency between one's expectations and one's reality.

Consistency in Expectation and Reality: The Case of Margaret Mahoney

Margaret Mahoney, aged fifty, worked as an assembler in a factory department. She had been on the job about eleven years, and during the interviews with the researchers she expressed very positive feelings toward her job, her coworkers, the company, and her boss. Here is a sample of her comments:

I love my work. It's a funny thing, it's a messy job, but I'm not happy when I'm not doing it. . . . I guess I just like to work with my hands. I like anything that's fast and with your hands. Then I'm not confined. I can stand or sit. If you're confined, like on machines, it's boring. I had a chance to go on grinders at 10 cents an hour more, but it's too confining. The ten cents doesn't mean that much.

Besides enjoying the content of her work, Margaret found her coworkers very congenial, and she enjoyed a high degree of acceptance in their social activities both within and outside the plant. Margaret was Irish-Catholic and her closest friends in the department were also Irish-Catholic women near her age, many of whom, like Margaret, were separated from their husbands or widowed. In her relations with coworkers, Margaret acted as an informal leader who initiated activities for others.

Margaret enjoyed working for the foreman of the department and spoke admiringly of him as well as of the company as a whole. She said:

You couldn't find a better boss in the United States. I couldn't pick any one thing out that makes him so good. He's fair, good, and he's not a slave driver. . . . You give him a fair day's work and he's fair.

Margaret had separated from her husband following an unhappy marriage. She had had five children and several grandchildren. Her family lived close by so that she saw them regularly. Margaret lived in a new house in a suburban development with an older brother. About her life outside the plant, Margaret had this to say:

I just love my house in the country. Everybody said I'd be scared living way out in the woods but I'm not. I always wanted to live in the country because I love gardening and hiking. Everybody says I have a green thumb, just like my father. I keep looking at the calendar to see when spring comes. I can hardly wait.

Everything in my house is so nice and new. I just love it. I've never been so contented in my life.

I see my children and grandchildren. I just love them and they're crazy about me, too. I'm happy and contented.

I would like to stay home and putter around. People tell me I wouldn't know what to do with my time, but I could find plenty to do. But I couldn't afford to stop work.

The note of contentment contained in these comments suggests an excessive degree of looking at the world with "rose-colored glasses." Yet they contain significant attitudes Margaret cultivated in her work and life situation and reflected her manner of dealing with experience. The contentment was based on a high degree of consistency between expectation based on status and experience and the social reality. There was little need for doubting her lot in life since she had been conditioned fully to live in the kind of social environment provided for her in the work and home situations.

The effect of this "goodness of fit" between expectations and reality is even more noteworthy in its capacity to compensate for deprivations in other spheres of life. The individual like Margaret Mahoney accepts deprivation, on the whole, with little assumption of responsibility. The experience of being "at one" with the social environment provides the basis for acceptance of deprivation because the social reality provides substitute supports and gratifications. This last observation will become clearer as we examine pertinent aspects of Margaret's personal history.

Unlike Richard Carleton, Margaret came from a large family. She was the youngest child and the object of much attention in the family. In her own words, she said:

My mother died when I was three years old. My oldest sister looked after me. I guess I was the spoiled one. My brothers and sisters catered to me a lot. I would go into tantrums if I didn't get what I wanted. My sister was strict with me. I had to be in by a certain time and all that. I wanted to be on my own. They screamed and hollered when I wanted to get married when I was 18, but I wanted to get on my own.

When I got married, I didn't know how to even cook because everybody had done things for me. I wanted to get on my own. But I learned it wasn't so nice. After I was separated my brothers and sisters helped me out, so it worked out O.K. My brother down south used to send me a check for $50 now and then. I guess they felt sorry for me and the kids.

The presence of supportive figures who could help Margaret "pick up the pieces" following her unhappy experiences compensated for the deprivations. At the same time this reliance on family beyond her childhood and adolescence also served to maintain her dependency on others. In Margaret's case, unlike Carleton, the dependency gratifications she received posed no conflict. As a woman in her particular culture, the maintenance of a dependent position was legitimate, and one of the important functions of the parental family. Besides its legitimacy for a woman, the dependency status seemed consistent in a case where there is unity between the individual and the social environment. Just as Margaret could maintain dependency in her relationships with brothers and sisters, so could she maintain this dependency in her work situation where behavior patterns were styled according to the status one had. There were enough other persons with whom she could share her status that little pressure existed for her to make decisions or to act out of difficult choices and commitments.

Reliance on the social environment for important ego functions is a special feature of consistency between one's status and expectations, on the one hand, and the social reality, on the other. Little conscious thought needs to be given by the individual to himself and his identity. It is prescribed within the matrix of social relationships. And as the individual changes in status with increasing age and family positions, the adjustments for the individual are made relatively easily. All this "fitting" holds true as long as the individual is congruent in all respects with his social environment, and as long as he is willing to accept the particular niche allotted for him.

The issue of "goodness of fit" and consistency between expectation and reality exists quite apart from the particular social class in which the individual experiences his development. In the illustration just cited, Margaret Mahoney experienced her development in a city within the upper-lower social class of the Irish-Catholic family and community. The same generalizations would hold for the upper-class Brahmin who lives his entire life in one social setting. Of course, the content of the individual's life varies considerably depending on his social class. Yet the important element of reliance on the social environment is a characteristic of consistency in expectation and reality regardless of social class.

In the comparisons between Richard Carleton and Margaret Mahoney, I have shown the differences in response between an individual who experiences discontinuity of expectation and reality and one whose inner and outer worlds are highly consistent. I should like now to direct attention to the different kinds of discontinuities found in modern work settings and how they are manifested. The obvious discontinuity worth studying next is the case of upward mobility.

DISCONTINUITIES IN UPWARD MOBILITY

Modern industrial society, particularly in the United States, is relatively open in that it provides opportunity for individuals to move upward in the socioeconomic hierarchy. The doors to upward mobility are to be found largely in the educational system. Here, able individuals prepare for careers and in doing so leave behind the social setting in which they were raised. In leaving this social setting behind, however, the upwardly mobile individual may soon experience anxiety and guilt to the degree that they finally impair his capacity to work and enjoy life. This outcome is not inevitable, but one that is frequently found in business, government, education, and the professions where the mobile individual works.

The anxiety experienced by the upwardly mobile individual largely comes from internal conflicts generated within his own personality. On the one hand, there is the driving and pervasive need to prove himself as assurance of his adequacy as a person; on the other hand, the standards for measuring his adequacy come from sources somewhat unfamiliar to him. He tends to exaggerate the relevance of behavior of individuals within the new social class to which he aspires and simultaneously builds up the qualities of these new models while he deprecates the adequacy of the inner values and performances derived from his past. Under these conditions, the upwardly mobile individual may feel as though he were on a treadmill from which there appears to be no escape. No degree of achievement, however much valued in work and social circles, serves to quiet the anguish and torment to which he subjects himself. Even in moments of leisure the tension may be maintained particularly if the anxiety sweeps the entire family and results in compulsive social climbing.

In other words, whereas the individual who "fits" takes many things for granted, the upwardly mobile individual frequently questions and weighs the correctness and adequacy of his own behavior and that of his family. Not being able to permit himself the almost reflexive action necessary in ordinary social interchange results in a massive energy drain and, in the extreme case, breakdown.

The second emotional element in the discontinuity experienced frequently in upward mobility is the burden of guilt. The issue of guilt is summed up in Thomas Wolfe's phrase, "you can't go home again." The upwardly mobile individual knows this fact, but finds it difficult to accept in the face of the unfinished business of the past. Particularly relevant in this regard is his deep feeling that he has more, and accomplishes more, than the important figures from his past whom he once loved and then left in his movement upward in the professional and social hierarchy. The feelings of guilt associated with higher achievement and material advantage than his father, in the case of the man, must be resolved and overcome. The sense of wholeness and adequacy as a person depends upon the success of this resolution.

Yet this need to overcome the burden of guilt is not easily accomplished, particularly if it contains the overtones of earlier guilt reactions in the comparison of self with one's father. Freud demonstrated the significance in normal development in infancy of the competitive feelings aroused in the male child in relation to his father. He referred to this competition, and the attendant guilt and anxiety, as the Oedipus complex. Freud indicated that the resolution of the Oedipus complex, and the competition for the wife-mother as love object, occurs in part through the identification with the father: "If I can not displace him, I will try to become like him." This formula of identification implies that the young child delays gratification of wishes and takes his own father as a role model whom he tries to imitate. Should this dynamic of identification actually develop, the child is then in a position to learn from his father and to use his father's standards as ideals to guide his achievement.

Clearly, however, in the case of upward mobility the child-adult does not identify fully with his own father. In fact, present in his own climb upward may be a rejection of his father as an object of identification. In the course of either leaving or rejecting his father, residues of guilt may continue to plague the upwardly mobile individual. His comparisons with other ideals, or models, may be overlaid with the earlier burden of guilt. It may well be that the guilt acts to accelerate the individual's desires for achievement as though he must continue to surpass and overcome the authority figures in his adult life who stand, psychologically speaking, in the place of his own father. The achievements may indeed be secured, but the inner sense of accomplishment and self-esteem may remain tenuous if not completely absent.

The life themes associated with upward mobility form an important part of the experience in the United States. These themes, described above, are among the favorites of novelists, including the late American writer, John P. Marquand, who characterized the movement upward as beyond "the point of no return."

Earlier, I distinguished the discontinuities of downward and upward mobility by the emotions of shame and guilt, respectively. This distinction is worth exploring further since shame and guilt pose two different and generally painful ways of experiencing the self.

Shame and Guilt

In feeling of shame, the individual senses that he is exposed to the view of others in a rather helpless and passive state. Actually, how others see him bears little on the causes of the feelings of shame. Their impetus comes from unconscious conflicts that use current life dilemmas as their vehicles of expression. You will recall the notes of shame and helplessness expressed in the comments of Richard Carleton. These existed apart from overt evaluations from his coworkers and fellows in the community. The shame found active expression over failing to realize in life the kinds of ideals in position, activity, and status that he had accepted internally in his early background and development. At a more unconscious level of experience, the shame echoed in Carleton's passive attitudes and dependence upon women. He identified with the suffering woman largely through experience with his mother but this identification carried over later in life in his relationship to his wife, who existed for him as a mother-surrogate. The sense of impending discovery of one's self as an inadequate, helpless male leaves the individual fearful and in a constant state of tension. The experience of downward mobility, of failure in achievement, carries these more basic unconscious conflicts, doubling the severity of the pain of the individual's existence.

In the case of guilt and upward mobility, the problematic issue in the individual's existence is whether he is truly entitled to the achievements and position that he apparently enjoys. Dynamically speaking, in the individual's unconscious there exist the earlier wishes to excel and be superior to an admired father, and at the same time the punitive guilt surrounding such wishes. Guilt does not follow a sense of helplessness, but rather of having entertained and even carried out in fantasy the wish to destroy a rival.

The tragedy of James Forrestal, the first U.S. Secretary of Defense, is instructive in this regard.[2] Forrestal exemplified in his

[2] See A., Rogow, *James Forrestal, A Study of Personality, Politics, and Policy*, (New York: The Macmillan Company, 1963).

life both the possibilities and problems of upward mobility and the struggle with guilt. After his graduation from Princeton he severed ties with his parents and early family experience as he pursued the responsibilities and rewards of, first, Wall Street and, then, government circles in Washington. His ultimate demise followed the projection of self-hatred outward in the form of paranoia and its redirection inward leading to suicide.

The distinction between shame and guilt and its connection with different forms of discontinuities in status is worth keeping in mind. The basic forms of discontinuity discussed so far have been downward and upward mobility. These forms probably exist as extremes in industrial society and as such serve to define the prototypes of the psychological conflicts in the disparity between expectation and reality.

As indicated previously, other types of discontinuity with similar but generally less severe effects can be observed in the various positions in organizations that stand at the boundaries of groups and their environment.

POSITIONS AT THE BOUNDARY AND
DISCONTINUITIES IN STATUS

A position at the boundary consists of a set of activities and responsibilities that place the individual in the role of mediating between different groups or organizations. Such positions increase in number as a society becomes more complex with larger organizations and an increased specialization of activity.

Earlier I mentioned the attention social scientists have given to the job of the foreman as an instance of a form of tension connected with a particular occupation. Social scientists sometimes referred to the dilemmas of this position as the "man in the middle" syndrome, referring, of course, to the fact that the foreman works between two quite different worlds. The first is the world of his work group with its elaborate social organization and informal codes of behavior. This social organization serves as a protective cocoon and mediates between the group and the outside authority figures.[3] The foreman may be all too keenly aware of this social organization, but he is not a part of it. Neither is he a part of the management group represented by the higher authority figures who set the standards of performance by which he and his work group will ultimately be evaluated. He must mediate between the demands of higher management and the conservative tendencies of group behavior. Lacking acceptance from and identification with either of these two worlds can frequently lead to the feelings of shame and helplessness that we find so characteristic of the downwardly mobile individual who in his own eyes fails to achieve his own internal expectations and ideals. I have come to the conclusion from observations that foreman and other "men in the middle" in the industrial work structure who are effective on their jobs manage to overcome the feelings of helplessness and shame through their own sense of competence and capacity to control outcomes. They do not accept the passivity of the in-between position, but instead seek actively to communicate standards of performance to their work groups as well as the realistic problems of performance to higher levels of management. Such an active posture is a crucial necessity for these positions and demands at the outset a core sense of self-esteem. Wise management knows how to support and reinforce this active posture with the assurance that strong "men in the middle" contribute immeasurably to the success of the enterprise.

While these active types never become accepted and integral members of the informal social organization, they do not aspire to such membership. They are content with achieving the respect of their subordinates and with maintaining a reputation for equitable management of human relations on the job.

Another type of position at the boundary fraught with potential conflict for the individual is that of salesman. The sales representative stands between his own organization whose products and services he represents and the customer's organization. He

[3] Chapter 7 will consider the psychological foundations of group formations in industry in some detail.

somehow has to identify with both organizations and mediate between their respective demands and needs.

Several years ago, I supervised a study of the problems of morale and productivity of a group of salesmen located in the district sales office of a large industrial organization. Responses of salesmen during interviews, and observation of their behavior on the job including contacts with customers, provided vivid illustrations of the psychological tensions growing out of conflicting statuses and evaluations.

By and large, the salesmen experienced indications of high status in their contacts with customers, but in their dealings within their own organization the opposite condition existed. This disparity in status held special meaning for the more experienced salesmen simply because their aspirations and expectations were considerably higher than those of the junior salesmen.

The salesman was a significant figure in the customer's office since the products sold generally were raw materials citical in the operations of the customer's business. The products, in many cases, accounted for a significant percentage of the costs, and questions of price, quality, and delivery dates were matters of serious discussion between the salesman and several key individuals in the customer's organization. (It was not unusual for salesmen, many of whom had good technical backgrounds, to sit in on staff discussions and to work with top executives individually in their calls on customers.)

Customer contacts were gratifying to the salesmen and contrasted sharply with general reactions within their own organization. Salesmen generally had to initiate contacts within their own company. Few persons, including their immediate supervisor, called upon them to review and discuss field matters relevant to the setting of marketing policies and programs. They usually learned about new programs in large meetings where they were passive recipients of information. Salesmen reported with considerable anger their embarrassment upon learning from customers, or the newspapers, of important changes affecting their product and its applications.

The salesmen also treated their physical surroundings in their office as symbolic of a relatively devalued position within their own organization. Located in a crowded building, old and musty in atmosphere, the salesmen had desks in a kind of bullpen arrangement and had little opportunity for private conversation. They considered it unthinkable, for example, to invite customer representatives to visit them for business conferences in their own offices.

The tensions aroused as a result of status inconsistencies were expressed in the form of anxiety about the future and self-doubt in their chosen work. Salesmen voiced many anxious complaints about the vagueness of their future and their inability to visualize where the job would lead in the years ahead. For most of the salesmen, even those with college degrees in engineering, the potential enjoyment in their work was associated with interacting with other people, rather than in pure technical problem solving. In the case of their job-related interactions, the differences in their experiences within and outside their own organizations led to conflicting self-evaluations and consequently self-doubt.

If left to his own devices, an individual who doubts himself and his adequacy typically becomes hypersensitive about status connotations in his everyday experiences. Questions of being included or excluded, accepted or rejected, are attached even to the most inconsequential events he encounters. This type of individual becomes obsessed with status symbols even to the point of believing and acting as though these symbols *cause* competence rather than the idea that individuals who act competently frequently receive various kinds of recognition for their performance. The status symbols as superficial forms of recognition then become the objects of attention, thinking, and striving, and deflect energy from the important substance of work.

No more moving portrayal of this problem of self-doubt and the confusion over status symbols is available than in the characterization of Willy Loman in Arthur Miller's *Death of a Salesman*.[4] Willy believed in and also acted on the fantasy that per-

---

[4] Arthur Miller, *Death of a Salesman* (New York: Viking Press, 1958).

sonal acceptance secured through status symbols is the route to job success. In living this fantasy, Willy became increasingly alienated from those who loved him and even from himself and his simpler dispositions. (The fact that Miller chose to portray this human struggle in the setting of the salesman's world was not a random artistic choice.)

The problem of the salesman who lives at the boundary of several social realities is to grasp and maintain a sense of himself and his relatedness to things that genuinely matter. The tendency for this boundary position to evoke contradictory signals as to where one belongs and how one is to evaluate himself makes this job particularly vulnerable to self-doubt and inconsistent self-evaluations.

Before concluding this chapter on the psychological meaning of status inconsistencies, there is another type of related problem worth our attention. This problem not infrequently acts as the Achilles' heel of individuals who achieve prominent positions of leadership in our society. I am referring to the condition of the leader whose self-evaluation is considerably more modest than the esteem in which he is held by other persons. I am not referring to false or feigned modesty, but instead to the genuine condition found among some leaders in various fields who never quite believe the evident importance they have assumed for others. It is not that they suffer from a lack of self-esteem as in the other types of conditions discussed in this chapter. Their self-evaluations are realistic, yet spiced with the humorous and even bizarre possibilities in life. Where once they aspired, if only unconsciously, for an apparently simple existence, they seem to find themselves at the center of movement in their chosen fields. If Shakespeare's formula on greatness contains any truth—"Some are born great, some achieve greatness, and some have greatness thrust upon them"—the case in point is the dilemma of the leaders who experience greatness as a condition external to their own dreams and aspirations.

The opposite case is that of individuals who assume leadership out of a sense of destiny, as though their position in life had been preordained; these individuals offer little resistance to accepting the esteem of others. In fact, the esteem offered by others makes little difference to this "born" leader. He is already sufficiently endowed with narcissistic qualities to require adoration from others. This type of leader risks his sense of reality in accepting all too readily an attitude of destiny and omnipotence. In the extreme, he may become psychotic and be overcome with delusions of grandeur.

The leader who has greatness "thrust upon him" may become impaired in his actions through a desire to act out his disbelief of his position in life. His ambivalence becomes apparent to others and may confuse his own actions as well as his communications with others. On the other hand, endowed with a sense of humor and a strong reality sense, the "reluctant" leader may come to understand the qualities that others value and may learn to use himself in highly effective ways.

Summary and Conclusion

An individual's sense of self-esteem is a hard-won result of his development. The way he experiences himself is generally consistent with the types of evaluations he receives from others. There exist, however, conditions in which the individual's statuses or evaluations from others represent marked discontinuities with his own evaluations and expectations. The extremes of these discontinuities are to be found in the conditions of downward and upward social mobility. Between these extremes, however, lie certain conditions in which discontinuities affect the individual but may lack the all-pervasive quality of downward and upward mobility. The "in-between" conditions are found frequently in those positions in organizations and professions that stand at the boundary of several social realities. One position at the boundary is that of the foreman who has received much attention as the "man in the middle." Another is the salesman who on the whole has not been the subject of serious consideration in the psychological study of work and career. Still another position at the boundary subject to disparities in status and self-evaluation is that of the leader who achieves prominence in the eyes of others.

The psychological difficulties of the individual in one or another of these conditions vary. The inner experiences of shame, doubt, anxiety, and guilt can be identified with particular types of discontinuity. The main object of this chapter has been to show these connections. Yet I should not leave the impression that the connections can be made in a rigid way. Any particular individual in a condition of discontinuity may experience the full range of these different emotions. What they all have in common, however, is their quality of pain.

The fact that an individual living in a condition of discontinuity experiences pain is by itself no cause to conclude that he suffers from a fixed and irreversible pathology. Another way of looking at pain is in its possibility for self-examination and insight. Socrates once said that a life unexamined is a life not worth living. Out of pain and self-examination may come brilliant achievement and creativity.

7 / Group Formations in Industry

Events in recent years have led to a renewed interest in the condition of the industrial worker. The central concern is the question of alienation. Have the technological and social conditions of work produced a class structure in which lower strata members exist apart from the main sources of vitality and commitment in our society?

The symptoms are subtle. America can boast of a high standard of living, yet there is substantial evidence of persistent pockets of poverty with the fear that those afflicted are least able to help themselves. We have a renewed interest in morality and aesthetics, yet there is an underlying fear of senseless violence, gang warfare, alcoholism, and drug addiction. The centers of pathology are the cities, the sprawling urban complexes that are merging one with the other, and producing some of the best and worst examples of the human condition.

Emile Durkheim, the nineteenth-century French sociologist, enlightened the study of social problems by describing a condition he called *anomie*—a state of individual rootlessness and detachment from society. The detachment is not self-chosen. It comes about through a variety of forces, including the breakdown in the division of labor through technological change, the weakening of the family, and the effects of social groupings in crowded cities.

From my experience in the study of factories and work groups it seems improbable that the bad social conditions present today come about in the aftermath of anomie. Anomie may well exist, but it is generally preceded by a structure of tightly organized groups that act in opposition to the dominant concerns of the middle classes. In the group organizations, the individual merges into the group as a response to some of the problems of personal development. It gives the person something to belong to, but nothing out of which he may grow. It sustains, but does not renew the person by presenting him with an issue of personal identity.

There are two constellations of ideas and beliefs that dominate the formation of these group structures. One exists around the fear of authority, a product of personal history that establishes bonds of relationship among individuals. The second is the fear of uncertainty growing out of a sense of helplessness in controlling the environment. How these two sets of fears come to dominate and color the formations of groups in industry is the subject of this chapter.

The approach I want to use in developing this subject is the case study. My colleagues and I at the Harvard Business School conducted a study in depth of a group of workers in a factory in a large eastern city.[1] Prior to that study, I had reported on two other investigations of behavior in industry[2] and along with the work of other researchers we had available a reasonably substantial base of data against which to test the generality of our findings. Subsequent work has also added to the experience I shall use in this chapter.

This case study enlightens the question of group formations in

[1] A. Zaleznik, C. R. Christensen, and F. J. Roethlisberger, with G. C. Homans, *The Motivation, Productivity, and Satisfaction of Workers: A Prediction Study* (Cambridge: Division of Research, Harvard University, Graduate School of Business Administration, 1958).

[2] A. Zaleznik, *Worker Satisfaction and Development* (Cambridge: Division of Research, Harvard University Graduate School of Business Administration, 1956). Zaleznik, *Foreman Training in a Growing Enterprise* (Cambridge: Harvard University Graduate School of Business Administration, 1951).

industry with a view from the inside. Most inquiries work from the outside, but in the course of doing so lose the dynamic point of view, that is, the connection among many complex factors that operate in situations. The view from the inside stresses the connection between how people feel and how they act. It looks for the effects of unconscious motivation and the symbolic meaning of events to deepen our understanding of how and why people act in work situations.

THE CASE STUDY

The workers at the center of this study were employed in a medium-sized factory located in the heart of a large city. While the company had a history of past success, it had fallen into more difficult times and had had several changes of management before we arrived at the plant. When we started the study employment had stabilized after several years of "shakedown."

Besides being employed in this company, the workers belonged to a union affiliated with a large international labor organization. The local union acted as an autonomous body calling on the international for assistance rather infrequently. The union shortly after the study began resolved an intense jurisdictional dispute that led to an election and new international affiliations. I witnessed the final stages of the turmoil connected with this dispute, but it too settled down early in the study.

The Workers

The fifty people in the group, of whom about one-third were women and two-thirds men, produced component parts and assembled them into units later incorporated in a large machine installation. The jobs ranged from simple, relatively unskilled machine and assembly operations to some fairly complex procedures, including set-up work and precision machining. The workers ranged in age from the early twenties to the sixties, and not all were married. There was a substantial number of single persons and survivors of marriages that had terminated through death or separation.

With few exceptions, the workers were born in the United States. Most of them were first-generation Americans whose parents had emigrated from European countries. The dominant ethnic group in the community, the factory, and this particular group was Irish, although there were Italians, Greeks, and eastern Europeans represented. A few of the workers were "Yankees" who came from rural backgrounds and could count several generations of their family background in the United States.

The City

Most of the workers called the city their home. They lived in crowded surroundings in the midst of a typically large family group. The ethnic divisions in the factory reflected the composition of the city where particular areas were identified with Irish or Italian family groups.

With roots in urban life, the workers in the department were governed to a marked extent by three important institutions: the family, the church, and the political party. There were strong family ties with the mother playing an important role in maintaining family stability and meeting the crises arising from illness, death, separation, and economic depression. America is known for its geographic mobility. Sons and daughters seldom remain near their parental families. This mobility, however, is more related to the class structure of the United States. The middle classes who fill the professional and executive ranks tend to be mobile. In the lower-income groups there is limited geographic movement. Among the workers in this study the dominating feature was proximity to their family of origin, church, and community.

The Roman Catholic Church strongly influenced the lives of the workers. Many had been educated in parochial schools and had identified themselves with a particular parish. When crises arose in the family, and there were many, church agencies provided medical and financial help as well as the basis for accepting deprivation and disaster. In its role as educator, the church inculcated values and beliefs that were important influences in the way the individuals organized their ideas about life.

As for the political party, the congested city with its immigrant population established an important base for the development of a hierarchy strongly allied to the Democratic Party. There were powerful party bosses and strong allegiances that were earned through the concrete help the party provided during periods of crisis in the family and the community.

The political organization not only helped in time of need, but also provided for positions in the power structure of the community. Ambitious individuals could work for the party and try to achieve influence in affairs. In a city with a history of rivalry between Yankee and Irish, with its limited mobility opportunities, the political arena became an effective one for assuming leadership. That the workers valued highly political influence was attested to by the prestige given to jobs on the police force, the fire department, and other city offices. Workers who left the factory for city jobs were viewed with considerable respect because members in the group believed that these jobs were not for the asking but depended on political influence.

Community, political, and church influences were centered around the major ethnic divisions. The Irish were dominant in the city because they outnumbered other ethnic groups. Yet because of geographic concentration, the various ethnic groups had their particular sphere of influence. The ethnic concentrations were easy to identify around important holidays and events. The Irish mobilized themselves around the celebration of St. Patrick's Day and centered the festivities in their community. Similarly, the Italians took the occasion of Columbus Day to reaffirm their group loyalties, while the Yankee community used the holidays of the American Revolution as well as the society pages to make visible their heritage and claims for continuing influence.

Needless to say, the ethnic divisions were the subject of competitiveness and rivalry in the city. The main feuds revolved around the Yankee-Protestant and Irish-Catholic groups, and the Irish and Italian groups. These feuds spilled over into places of employment and were evident in group relations in the factory. Struggle for control of the union, for example, went on between the Irish who worked in the operating departments of the plant, and the Italians who dominated the inspection departments. The Yankee and Irish contentions were reflected in the relationship between management and the workers, although interestingly enough the Yankee influence had never really been strong in the management of the company. At the time of the study the ownership of the company was Jewish, although the management at middle levels was Yankee if we take this group to reflect a diffuse Protestant affiliation and not necessarily the descendants of the early settlers.

Social Background, Personal History, and Levels of Aspiration

As a result of a series of intensive interviews, we were able to grasp the connection between the workers' motivation and their background and history. The striking connection was the relatively low level of aspiration as a consequence of experience that generated rigid attitudes about what it takes to get ahead and the meaning of life in a complicated environment.

About 75 per cent of the workers had social orientations which were basically rooted in their class. The so-called upper-lower class backgrounds were characterized by low aspirations for mobility and identification around family, church, and ethnic group. The members showed strong dependency needs, the need for security in the face of their histories of hardship, and a strongly ambivalent attitude toward authority. The acquiescence to and dependence upon authority were directed toward family, church, and political bosses. The suspicion and fear of authority were evident in attitudes toward management.

The workers' world was a highly moral one in the sense that they held strong beliefs about right and wrong. For example, any behavior which appeared disloyal to the group was considered bad; or, failure to help a person in need was viewed as morally wrong. The group frowned upon openly frugal attitudes and behavior. It was acceptable for a person to "put away for a rainy day," but beyond that, saving, especially if it meant careful expenditures or a "tight" attitude, seemed strange.

Codes of conduct operated on a double standard. A man was permitted to be carefree, but a married woman was expected to be serious. Sexual promiscuity was not condemned for the man, but was a serious violation for the woman. Women expected to be treated deferentially, extending their family rights into the work situation. As one male worker put the case in criticizing openly crude behavior in the presence of women, "After all, the woman he talks to might be somebody's wife or sister."

The remaining 25 per cent of the workers were "out of line" in social background. This group expressed values different from those of the majority of workers. They felt superior to others and independent. Many of the workers with "out-of-line" backgrounds were Yankees and had been raised in rural communities. In their case, being in the factory in the first place represented to them a "comedown" in life.

The summaries of the personal histories of the workers presented a startling picture. The stories were replete with the hardships endured in immigrant families trying to make their way in the city. The instances of deprivation and emotional insecurity left relatively few individuals unscarred.

Only 20 per cent of the workers in the department could report histories free from unusual or serious economic, social, or emotional blows. Deprivations occur to all human beings, but not necessarily inconsistent with their stage of development and position in the life cycle. Almost 40 per cent of the workers, for example, experienced events of sufficient severity during early childhood to place extra burdens in meeting the ordinary tasks and conflicts of life. These deprivations consisted of death, illness, divorce or separation, unemployment of parents, and other dislocations occurring during childhood and early adolescence.

These histories suggested a break in the bonds of love and affection, and the loss of stable objects with whom the individuals could identify and borrow strength during the formative years.

The third group of workers, a little over 40 per cent, experienced serious events like divorce, illness, death of spouse, and so on, but these occurred after adolescence at a time when the individual could utilize various institutional sources of help like the church and public agencies. This ability to use help does not minimize the severity of the situations, but should be distinguished from the kinds of deprivations that occur when the person is most dependent, during the preadolescent periods of life.

The types of background and history experienced affected the workers' attitudes, particularly their aspirations. The majority, about 65 per cent, indicated no aspirations beyond reasonable security and consistency in their environment. They had no desire for social leadership or for job mobility. In other words, they viewed themselves largely as "followers." About a quarter of the workers, mainly men, expressed hopes for job advancement along craft or technical lines, and the remainder, about 10 per cent, expressed the aspirations of the social leader in plant and community activities. Such leadership aspirations were centered around organizations like the Holy Name Society, Knights of Columbus, veterans' organizations, and the political party. None of the workers expressed any aspiration for work leadership or supervisory jobs.

In the relationship between background and motivation, most of the workers were "in line" with respect to past experience and present social situation. Most of them had experienced personal blows either in childhood or in adulthood and consequently had at one time or another been forced to seek aid through institutions in the community. They were products of the problems that accompany immigration, life in a large city, poor health, and economic depressions.

Most of the workers never knew one another before coming to work in this department. While they had much in common in their social background and personal history, there were still important differences among them. They differed in sex, age, family status, and ethnic background. While the dominant ethnic group was Irish, there were other groups represented with differing orientations, such as Italian, Polish, Greek, Armenian, Jewish, and Yankee. Many of the workers could speak with pride about working in a "Little League of Nations" and could state warmly that a person's nationality made no difference in worker relationships. But at another level, the ethnic differences were important because they had to be "lived with" just as the workers had to live with such differences as age, seniority, education, and sex. They were conscious of these differences, but quite unaware of just *how* they were managing to live with them.

This group of workers came into a factory which, like all other factories, was highly structured. The jobs they were to do, the materials they were to work with, the machines they were supposed to use, their expected output, were all fixed by specialists who planned the most efficient order of work. They were expected to turn out a "fair day's work for a fair day's pay," observe the rules of employment, e.g., starting and stopping on time. They were given rest periods and were expected to maintain a reasonable pace of work all day with no loitering on the job. Any complaints could be channeled into the union-management grievance procedure.

All of these prescribed methods of work and rules of employment were designed to meet the economic purposes of the organization which in the long run were important to both management and the workers. Yet the behavior of the workers involved a complex social process unanticipated in the strictly technical and economic arrangements of work.

A Working Day

This elaborate social process, a product of group formation, was woven into the fabric of work, evident most clearly in the rhythm of a typical working day.

A first glance upon arriving at the department shows nothing out of the ordinary. Men and women are at work at machines and benches. The air is filled with the noise of work: the clatter of boxes, the hum of motors, the scraping of tool against metal. But another sound reaches our ears. Men are shouting at each other, and soon a chorus of laughter swells up as though attempting to overcome the buzzing of the machines. Two men are arguing with each other. One man is saying derisively that "Italians don't know how to eat right. They stuff themselves full of spaghetti instead of good red meat." The other worker shouts back that no matter what the Italians eat they at least got Columbus Day declared a legal holiday, but the Irish still have to come to work on St. Patrick's Day. And so it goes. The laughter and shouting dies down and once again the sounds of work dominate. Soon a man leaves his machine and walks out of the department. As though this were a signal, two men rush over to his machine and leave a note in front of it. The worker returns, and picks up the note; his sheepish smile sets off the gales of laughter again.

If this were a Friday morning, the day following pay day, we would see before the start of the work day one or another of the workers circulating through the department, collecting slips and money and then drawing one slip from the hat. He would then turn the money over to a worker who would smile and take goodnaturedly the teasing about how lucky he is or how stingy he is in not offering to share his good fortune. For this particular person just won a weekly draw pool and instead of his fifty cents he got back ten dollars. Occasionally one or two other workers walk around to collect money and distribute it in a lump sum to one of the contributors.

But if we look further we see money being collected, but this time coins and sometimes a dollar bill are put through a slot into a box. On the box is a worker's name, and we are told that he has been out sick for two weeks, and this is a collection to help him out. "After all, he has three kids and you know what it's like with no paycheck." And so back to work with occasional glances up from the machine or bench as a man dressed in white shirt, tie, and jacket walks down the aisle shuffling papers in his hand and calling for the foreman who is talking with a worker. This man besides being dressed differently comes from another world, the office, and like any newcomer his presence is noticed.

Soon another stranger appears, in shirt and tie, with sleeves rolled up and pencils in his pocket. He is carrying a clipboard with papers attached and a gadget that looks like a stopwatch. He talks to the foreman and then walks over to a worker at his machine and begins scratching notes as he jiggles the stopwatch. He remains for about a half hour and then leaves, still writing notes and adding columns of numbers. As soon as he is gone, other workers rush up and ask questions.

The elevator carrying skids of metal parts stops at the department floor. A man steps out and talks hurriedly with a woman who works on the aisle. She in turn talks to other workers and soon the news is passed through the department that someone heard that someone in the office had told one of the foremen that there was going to be a layoff on the sixth floor, maybe ten people, maybe twenty, who knows. A stillness follows, and worried looks appear on faces, particularly on the faces of the workers who are low on seniority. One man, an elderly worker, reaches into his box and pulls out a bottle of pills and leaves for the washroom.

Soon a bell rings as a cart is pushed into the department. Men and women, some carrying boxes, rush to form a line to get coffee and doughnuts. Those carrying boxes get as many as five cups of coffee. They are runners and bring the coffee to small groups which cluster here and there about the floor. Men seem to group with men and women with women. There is a great deal of joking and arguing, particularly among the men. The topic of conversation varies from who on the city's major league baseball team gives the most generous tip to cab drivers to teasing one of the bachelors about his late date the night before.

If we look carefully around the department we notice, however, that some of the workers are not involved in these groups. Men sit alone here and there drinking coffee and staring into space or reading a newspaper. In one section of the floor men and women sit at a table drinking coffee, but they are silent, each absorbed in his own thoughts or perhaps exchanging a word or two with his neighbor. At the back of the room, seated in front of a machine as though overlooking the entire department, is a woman. Someone brings coffee to her and occasionally one or another of the workers stops by her machine to talk. But she never moves away from her machine to talk. Unlike the other workers who sit alone and are isolates, she is the informal leader of the department and one of the most popular and influential workers in the group.

The bell rings, signalling the end of the break. The pattern of work and occasional incidents of joking and interruptions with the appearance of a stranger continues until lunch time. Once again, this is the period for the formation of small groups around the department. Only this time, if we look carefully, we notice that the groupings are a little different from the ones we had observed during the coffee break. Men from one coffee group join with men from another to play cards and women from different sections of the department cluster together for their card game. Some people leave the department together to go to the cafeteria. And, as before, some men and women sit alone eating their lunch, occasionally getting up from their chairs to stare out the window.

Let us pause here to examine what we have observed. In our brief visit, we have seen just about every type of behavior which made up the work and social life in the department. If we were to stay for a period of six months or longer, we would find this behavior recurring day after day with the same people involved in the same activities with others. The fact that this behavior persists makes it important to the actors and for us to understand.

We can classify the behavior in the department into four categories: first, work behavior; second, joking or horseplay; third, limited social activity; and fourth, extended social activity. Each category involves a certain kind of relationship among workers, with certain codes of conduct and with an important meaning to individuals and the group. When taken as a whole, the behavior patterns form the human context in the factory.

Work Behavior

The outstanding fact about the work behavior is its solitary nature. Each worker is on his own in doing his work despite the fact that the modern technology out of which the work organization is forged implies a high degree of specialization and interdependence. Each worker in effect performs a series of operations which are later added to by other workers until the final product is formed. If one worker fails to perform his work satisfactorily, the chain is broken and the effects are felt in amount of output and in customer satisfaction. But in terms of awareness, there is little feeling of interdependence of activity. The worker's concept of the job is narrowed down to his immediate task which is repetitive and technically isolated. Therefore, in talking about his job, one worker reflects to us this sense of unrelatedness in the following way:

Some days you come in here you're full of pep and some days nothing looks good to you. If you have your mind on something else, the work doesn't get monotonous. When you do repetitive work, you can't concentrate on your work because it just gets too monotonous. . . . Today, I know what I'm going to be doing on Monday. I may not know the exact job number, but I know it will be the same kind of job. . . . If I went into another shop, I know it would only be a matter of time before it got monotonous. I'm not complaining about monotony, you understand, it's a fixture here. . . . Monotony is just something you have to put up with. It's like the sun coming up and the sun going down. I know it's going to come up in the morning and go down at night.

This sense of unrelatedness and lack of involvement in the job would quickly become intolerable if it were not for the social relationships which the workers had established with one another. These relationships appeared intrinsically satisfying in providing some human contacts. But at the same time the activities contained many reflections of tensions and even served to express aggression in manageable ways.

Joking and Horseplay

Those brief instances of joking relationships which I described do not convey the extent to which it dominated interpersonal relationships in the department. Men teased one another about ethnic background, personal habits, marital status, and work behavior. The group members felt joking was important to them and several workers explained its significance in this way:

We do a lot of joking around. You have to do it or else you go batty in a place like this.

Joking creates good feeling. Management tries to keep joking and horseplay at a minimum, but you still need it, or this job would be unbearable. . . . It makes us all feel good.

Everybody's riding each other all the time and kidding, especially X, he's a beaut. He's always on somebody's back but that is what makes it fun to work here because there's always something going on. It helps break the deadly monotony of these jobs. . . . We do a lot of joking about nationalities around here. I ride Y and Z, too. He's a Greek but we'll be riding him, and then next thing we'll be out together, so you can see it doesn't really mean anything too serious.

There are a lot of nationalities up here, and we let them know it. You know we got Jews and Turks and Arabs around here. If they can't take it, it's too darned bad. . . . But up here we gotta do some of this joking—if we don't what are we going to do to break up the monotony? Every once in a while, anybody gets called a lot of names that if you were called them on the outside you would punch the guy in the face, but in here, it's O.K. You sort of expect it. It's the kind of joking we do and everybody has to take their turn at it.

That joking relieves the tensions created by the monotony of the job provides one explanation with a certain validity. But if we kept a record of who participated in the joking and who initiated it this behavior takes on an added significance. For the most part, members of high-status groups initiated the joking on members of low-status groups. The codes of behavior demanded that the recipient accept the joking. He could reciprocate, and indeed was expected to, but he could not initiate or get angry at the jibes.

Earlier I pointed out that the men and women were strangers to each other before coming to work in the plant. The fact that they must work in the same department demanded at a minimum that they avoid conflict. Despite the uniformities in their social background, their differences in nationality and community loyalty became a source of uncertainty and potential conflict. The joking and horseplay created a ritualistic means of bringing the potential conflict to the surface, accepting it, and then allowing it to recede into the background. The ritual created sham conflict to avoid real conflict.[3] The joking had another meaning in relation to the problems of managing personal tensions. In observing the group I was struck by the rhythm of the behavior. It was as though in the course of working alone the individual became engaged in a kind of fantasy thinking that brought him close to the sources of personal anxiety. I assume that the anxieties were related to sexual and aggressive themes, since the interviews provided abundant evidence of the individual problems in managing wishes.

The joking had a distinctive aggressive coloration. By "staging" the dramatic play-out of aggressive behavior under the control of group codes the individual could detach himself from personal anxiety and tension, if only for a brief period of time. When work resumed, the build-up of anxiety seemed to begin again.

A few workers kept apart from these rituals and the life of the group. These were older men and women who had established a mutual relationship of avoidance as a reflection of their difference. As long as the individual abided by certain codes of conduct, the group seemed content to allow him to isolate himself.

[3] A. R. Radcliffe-Brown, *Structure and Function in Primitive Society* (Glencoe, Ill., Free Press, 1952).

Limited Social Activity

The third category of behavior, limited social activity, included all of the games and collections which involved interaction of very short duration. The activities in this category included primarily number pools, savings pools, collections. They took place generally the morning after pay day, involved a large number of workers, and had a special significance in the social life of the group.

Take first the number pools. This game was a form of lottery in which workers put in a small amount of money in exchange for a number. The winning number, either drawn from a hat or corresponding to the selected digit in the parimutuel horse racing report, determined which player took the pool. The amount of money involved was usually small, the bets ranging from 25 to 50 cents with winnings of about ten dollars. Some workers also placed number bets with bookies outside of work, but the games I am referring to here were those organized within the department. The number pools gained the widest participation of any activity in the department and, as a result, were important integrating rituals.

Here is how one worker explained what the pools meant to her:

Pools are good things. You always have the hope of winning the Friday pool money. . . . We used to get paid at two o'clock Friday afternoon. We'd have all our work done by that time, and then the fun would really start. After all week of digging and working away, we'd look forward to Friday afternoon. There must have been 10 pools going on at the same time—and the excitement! It was wonderful! It gave you something to look forward to and it was almost like a circus. It really made the week worth while.

The theme again was one of excitement, breaking up the routine and an event to be anticipated. But the pools meant more than just excitement. The workers' dream often centered around gaining a windfall—winning a large sum of money that for some would be their hope of "bailing out," for others their hope of luxury, even if only short lived. They could in the plant organize to make small windfalls possible so that the lucky winner could do a little something out of the ordinary such as buy a dress for his wife or have a night out. The fact that the betting rituals were of such short duration and involved passing money allowed anyone to join the game and in this sense created another basis for overlooking status differences.

The savings pools were also an organized windfall, but differed from the number pools in that every participant was guaranteed a windfall. A group of eleven workers each contributed a dollar for eleven weeks. They drew numbers from a hat and the winner collected eleven dollars. When a person won, he continued paying the dollar but was no longer eligible to draw. Consequently, at the end of eleven weeks each worker paid in eleven dollars and received in turn the same amount. Interestingly enough, women typically organized savings pools while men organized number pools. The women would urge men to join the savings pools so that they would be assured of a lump sum of money. One woman explained the importance of the savings pools to the men in this way:

> With the men, they take $1.00 a week out of their pay and their wife doesn't know about it. They then get the $11.00 all at once and the wife still doesn't know. Well, maybe they'll play cards with that extra spending money or maybe they'll take their wife out on an anniversary celebration. If a person's anniversary was coming up, he'd say to his wife, "I'm going to save $2.00 a week out of the pay to take you out." She wouldn't appreciate it, but with a surprise like that, by saving in the pool, why it's much nicer, so that's why the men want to come in. They seem to enjoy it a lot.

The collections were still another form of limited social activity in which the ritual permitted the visible expression of important life themes concerning deprivation and misfortune. A sickness, or death in the family, called for expressions of sympathy by providing concrete financial help. Group codes expected each worker to give, but the amounts varied depending on the individual's family situation. Women were expected to give more than men, but some contribution was in order for all. If a worker failed to contribute, he would get only a very small collection, if any at all, when misfortune struck him. On the other side, liberal contributors who were also popular received large collections. Whatever a person gave or received, he was participating in a ritual of deprivation, a life-theme intimately familiar to most of the men and women in the group.

Extended Social Activity

The nucleus of the group formations in the department grew out of the extended social activity during coffee breaks and lunch periods. The social interchange during these periods were of longer duration as compared with the pools and the collections, and the boundaries of each clique and subgroup were therefore more strongly marked.

It would take more space than is here available to show how the subgroups formed, with their membership and leadership patterns. The interested reader should turn to the detailed account of the case as it appears in *The Motivation, Productivity and Satisfaction of Workers: A Prediction Study*. I will summarize the main findings.

The basic subgroups expressed the differences in life stage of the individual around age and sex, with the ethnic differences as the central feature marking off status in the group. The dominant ethnic group, the Irish-Catholics, recreated in the social structure of the department the themes of family relationship and allocated roles to individuals accordingly. The unmarried man, no matter what his age, took the role of the "boy." He generally lived at home with his mother, or an older sister, and in a similar vein depended upon the women in the department to maintain the internal coherence of the group. He was permitted a relatively carefree life so long as he observed the demands of group cohesion, particularly in maintaining a stable relationship with outside authority figures.

The "men" in the group consisted of married men who had family responsibility. These men permitted the women to dominate the leadership of the group both internally and externally. (The group regularly elected its informal leader, a single woman, to the position of union treasurer.) In turn, they were permitted tension release activities in the forms described previously. And, as the earlier quote indicated, the women regulated the gaming so that winning and losing never got out of control.

The "women" consisted of the responsible, usually married women who exerted the most influence in the department. The "girls," on the other hand, were somewhat less responsible, usually unmarried, and engaged in a life-style more frivolous than that of the women.

Two other subgroups are worth mentioning here. These consisted of older workers who banded together into separate subgroups of men and women. These workers were grandparents in their family life and treated accordingly in the group.

In his beautiful study, *The Irish Countryman*, the anthropologist, Conrad Arensberg, reported a study of life in rural Ireland.[4] His description of the social structure, and the allocation of roles depending on age, sex, and family status paralleled observations of an American plant to a remarkable degree. The dominance of the Irish ethnic group in the department resulted in an extension of the family and community patterns into the factory. The way these extensions occurred could be seen most easily in the formation of the cliques around the extended social activity. The Irish workers permitted members of other ethnic groups to participate in some of the extended activities, but only in a marginal way. For example, one such activity consisted of a card game involving high-status Irish workers. This game drew many observers, including the younger "regulars," who were Irish but held junior positions in the social structure. The Italians and other minority ethnic representatives were also permitted to stand and watch the game, but they were not allowed to joke or to criticize the play.

In another case, the Italians could take subordinate roles in the

[4] Conrad Arensberg, *The Irish Countryman* (New York: The Macmillan Company, 1937).

conversation groups in which high-status Irish workers participated. This role demanded that the Italian, who was vying for
membership, be the steady coffee carrier. He regularly collected
the money, joined the coffee line, and brought the coffee to the
group.

I have presented in condensed form a description of the background and behavior of a group of factory workers. Other studies that my colleagues and I have conducted suggest that the
material presented is fairly typical of the group formations in
industry, particularly in urban centers with distinctive ethnic
divisions visible in the social structure of the community. I suggested in opening this chapter two main themes important in the
explanation of these group formations. These themes, representing the motivations of the individual growing out of his history
and experience, are: (1) the fear of authority and (2) the fear of
uncertainty.

THE FEAR OF AUTHORITY

The fear of authority as a common motivation among individuals in work groups is expressed most clearly in the practice of
restriction of output found as a regular feature in group life. The
group described in this chapter was no exception.

Group members held certain ideas about the amount of output
they were expected to produce as their part in a "fair day's work
for a fair day's pay." The expected output level hovered near the
standards set by management but tended to be correlated with
the individual's social position in the group. Low-ranking members who wanted to get along in the group pegged their output
below the level of "regulars." The "ratebusters" consisted of individuals with "Yankee-Protestant" backgrounds and with rural
upbringing, different from most of the group. The group referred to these individuals as "job killers" and viewed them with
hostility.

The practice of restriction of output acted as a mechanism for
regulating the group's relations with authority figures. The man-

agement, as a symbol of authority, was an object of suspicion and fear. In the eyes of the regular group members it was important to give the minimum expected output so that the authority figures could not criticize the group or take punitive action. At the same time the pegging of output kept individual productivity levels close to the average and made it difficult to single out any one individual as "better or worse." Authority figures would therefore find it difficult to differentiate individuals within the group for either special reward or punishment. The fact that "ratebusters" existed did not diminish the effect of the codes restricting output, at least in the minds of the group members.

The attitudes toward authority, as these led to group practices, acted as strong elements in maintaining group cohesion. The group controls on its members operated almost continuously, since the important element in the restrictive practices was the attitude of the individual. It made less difference how much an individual actually produced and turned in as compared with his acting as though he accepted fully the restrictive code. Workers could test this acceptance simply by watching how an individual worked and occasionally engaging him in a ritual of joking that served as a means of communicating mutual intent and attitude.

By and large, one could find little reality in the work of management to warrant the conclusion that these were malevolent figures. Yet the idea persisted and in fact is a general characteristic of work groups in industry. How can we account for this fear of authority?

The answer to this question resides in large part in the particular history and experience common in the lives of the urban worker. Most individuals have experienced ambivalent attitudes toward authority during their early experience in life. These attitudes tend to focus on the parents, but gradually the testing of reality in a good relationship with parents permits a modification. The individual tends to identify with authority through the eyes of his parents and to reorganize his perceptions more in accord with reality. He neither overestimates nor depreciates the power and competence in the hands of authority figures.

This educative experience is difficult to sustain under conditions where severe tensions and disruptions exist in family life. The absence of stable objects for identification, through death, separation, divorce, or the failure of parents to assume an active role in family affairs, shortcircuits the educative experience in development. The effect is to weaken the ego of the individual to the point where his fears of authority lead to excessive reliance on group formations for protection. The individual as a result is unable to exert initiative to assure in reality the potential benefits available through work and the development of his skills. A circular process occurs of increasing dependency on the group and a deepening of the fear of authority as life crises inflict pain upon the individual and his family. The tendency is to blame external authority for personal plight and deprivation, when the forces of life that inflict pain are largely impersonal and must be managed by the individual.

The Fear of Uncertainty

A second dominating motivational theme underlying the group formations described earlier is the fear of uncertainty. Given the painful experience of development common in the large city among lower-income families, the individual experiences anxiety with respect to his ability to control his own feelings and life situation. On the inner side, his own feelings revolve around aggression and anger in response to experiences in early development. In his relations with the environment, increasing perception of an arbitrary and uncontrollable environment heighten the aggression.

The responses of the individual vary. For some the route of escape through devices like alcohol appears. For others physical illness and complaints appear. Others abandon family responsibility and "take off" from their homes. Still others live within the culture of the group that supports and sustains, but seldom liberates the individual from his fears of uncertainty. The sustaining influence appears frequently in group ritual and myth that allows the individual to wish for the "windfall" or to believe in some sort of all-powerful influence that will liberate him from uncertainty. Not infrequently, the all-powerful influence is seen in the role of the political boss who makes escape real sometimes by producing the city job, one of the coveted positions in life.

The fear of uncertainty is expressed in other ways. Group members have generally a low tolerance for ambiguity. The worker who is "out of line," or from a different ethnic group, is viewed initially with some suspicion. Much of group ritual acts to reduce this ambiguity, to restore a condition of social certitude in the relations among men and women of different status and social background. While in the absence of these rituals open conflict might emerge, still one should not infer a contribution to the development of the individual in his capacity to deal with ambiguity and uncertainty.

ALTERNATIVES TO RESTRICTIVE GROUP FORMATIONS

I am not optimistic over possibilities for basic changes in the motivational condition of the adult who has had long experience in the work force. Many of the experiments in group participation and permissive management are concerned with finding ways of changing the restrictive group patterns. These approaches assume that change in group patterns will result in individual changes. The evidence on the whole is inconclusive. Temporary effects have been achieved as in the experiments at the Western Electric, and in the change experiments conducted by Kurt Lewin and his students.

These experiments indicate that group behavior patterns shift somewhat when individuals in the group identify with the experimenters and their purposes. These experimenters typically come from outside the organization and the authority structure. We are unable to judge, therefore, the effects on enduring group relationships.

Another view of these experiments indicates that they are mute with respect to effects on individual motivation at either the conscious or unconscious level of awareness. Ultimately, questions of new group formations must address the motivational issue directly. Recent evidence along these lines supports the more cautious and pessimistic view. More recent studies by Victor Vroom, for example, suggest that the response of the individual to participative techniques in management depends on his motivaton.[5] Where the individual has authoritarian and dependent attitudes like those described in this chapter, permissive management tends to induce added uncertainty and even anxiety.

Perhaps the greatest potential for change resides in the system and practice of education during the formative years. If the schools can teach individuals to test their basic attitudes, while teaching skills useful in the work world, then more enduring alterations may occur. In addition, our structure of education has to be alert and sensitive to the gifted individual no matter what his past experience and social background. The hard fact is that the gifted individual from the lower social classes may be ignored in our present educational practices.

The same recommendation may be made to managements of large industries: to look for the gifted individual in work groups and provide him with a workable alternative so that he can take advantage of the rewards of mobility. We should recognize, however, that in education and in industrial management a barrier to mobility exists in the hesitation of individuals to take steps that seem to require rupture of existing family and group identifications.

This barrier came home to me in an interview with a very gifted person who, in fact, was the informal leader of the work group described in this chapter. She had considerable talent in working with people and a great deal of intelligence. I asked her if she had ever considered any other jobs. She described the efforts of her teachers to have her continue her education and offers to take supervisory jobs. In all cases, she refused because of her unwillingness to take a step that she considered "crossing the

[5] See *Some Personality Determinants of the Effects of Participation* (Englewood Cliffs, N. J.: Prentice Hall, 1960).

line," moving outside the circle of her group. This decision involved considerable ambivalence as evidenced in the fact that she periodically became ill, with no determined physical basis for the illness. The illness seemed to express her mixed feelings in remaining with her group.

The interventions through education in the life of the individual and his group attachments inflict conflict and pain. Yet these feelings can be managed provided the alternatives are made real.

In those instances where little change appears likely in the conditions underlying the restrictive group formations, the guiding concepts of reciprocity, justice, and equity in human relationships may have to be more deeply utilized as compared with the more optimistic assumptions of participative management. In the long run, however, the test will be in the evidence offered by experience.

8 / *The Management of Power in Interpersonal Relations*

Much of modern organization theory has grown out of social science research on behavior in the industrial work group. These studies of group formations among the blue-collar workers shed considerable light on motivation and its relationship to productivity and job satisfaction. In contrast, few firsthand investigations of executives who are at the center of the power structure of organizations are available. As a result current organization theories appear lopsided, or at least incomplete.

Observation of executives shows they are no less engaged in complex interpersonal relationships than the blue-collar worker. The transactions are different, however, because they involve directly the uses and consequences of power. In the industrial work group, power in interpersonal relationships is less visible because it is relatively unavailable.

Power in organizations emanates from the top. It resides in the person and position of the chief executive of the corporation and represents a consolidation of historical forces within the person and the organization. One important job of a chief executive is to draw together the sources of influence residing in his position. The degree and quality of such influence depends on the history of the organization and the traditions left behind by predecessors.

Whether the traditions remain intact or are altered to form a new consolidation and use of power depends to a great extent on the personality dynamics of the incumbent.

Power transactions occur within an executive group, a collection of individuals whose position in the structure is like the arrangement of a group of stars in a constellation around a central figure. This executive constellation becomes the instrument for using power.

If the exercise of command seems essentially a lonely task it is because of this tendency for power to emanate from the central position of the chief executive. But we should not infer that the isolation resulting from how power is generated extends to isolation in how power is distributed and used to impel the work of the organization. The main function of the executive constellation is to make power meaningful, in terms of moving the organization along a path and to implement a strategy that is relevant to organizational effectiveness.

The study of interpersonal relations among executives requires, therefore, an analysis of the formation and workings of a power constellation. Power constellations differ in structure and function. The main differences can best be understood in the terms of the theory of personality dynamics. The engagement that executives experience in a constellation is far from accidental. It is an outcome of the ways they have learned to adapt as expressed in their styles of behavior, in their personal strengths and vulnerabilities, in their personal conflicts and anxieties, and how they need to use one another to pursue a life pattern. In short, the story of any power constellation is a human one seldom discussed in the analysis of executives' relations, but always in the backdrop of the staging of their performance.

Needless to say, power constellations vary in their effectiveness both as instruments of organization action and as personal settings for the individuals involved. Effective or ineffective executive performance relates in large measure to the qualities of the constellation. As these qualities permit or inhibit formulating and acting on strategies, the effects are seen in how the organization moves on and uses opportunities.

THE STRUCTURE OF POWER CONSTELLATIONS

The easiest place to look for evidence on the existence of power constellations is the most visible of all chief executive positions—the Presidency of the United States. Political scientists point out the fact that in one office, bound by a set of formulations in the constitution and visible precedents in the history of the office, we find marked variations in how the position is used. Richard E. Neustadt in his book *Presidential Power*[1] draws a number of sharp comparisons. Franklin D. Roosevelt employed in his use of power the artistry of ambiguity. He established multiple constellations in special and even competitive roles allocated to trusted advisers. Dwight D. Eisenhower employed the logics of organization with levels of authority and staff arrangements. His main power constellations centered in his relationships with Sherman Adams in the organization of the office, and with John Foster Dulles in foreign affairs. Where Roosevelt used ambiguity to assure his intimate involvement in the decisions of the nation, Eisenhower used organization rationality to establish distance between himself and the processes of action.

Students may differ on the explanation of the variations in approach to the same office of chief executive, but they agree on the fact that these variations have to be explained before we get a workable understanding of executive behavior. For some, the explanation is in the terms of the situation. Situationalists argue in the extreme that the conditions and problems "outside" differ so, the office of chief executive is not really the same. The problems that faced Franklin D. Roosevelt, for example, explain his use of ambiguity while those confronting Dwight D. Eisenhower account for his use of more formalized administration.

[1] Richard E. Neustadt, *Presidential Power* (New York: John Wiley and Sons, 1960).

Other students, like Neustadt, look for the personal dimension in explaining executive organizaton and action. It is the problem from the "inside," from within the chief executive, that is crucial to understanding.

The test of the argument is, of course, in examining the behavior of the individual over time as he moves from office to office and role to role. Did Eisenhower's style of leadership differ from the military to the Presidency? Probably not enough to support the position of the "situationalists."

Woodrow Wilson, whose case I shall discuss in more detail later in this chapter, exercised power within a two-person constellation with Colonel House. John F. Kennedy also utilized the "pairing" in that the working relationship most central to how he used power existed in the confidence he shared with his brother Robert Kennedy.

The shifting structure of the power constellations in government is also evident in a rapid scanning of leadership succession in the Soviet Union. Joseph Stalin existed in a kind of patriarchal constellation in which he was the central figure with subordinates equally dispersed under his autocratic control. Upon his death, reaction emerged in the form of criticism of the "cult of personality." Khrushchev, who himself did much to bring discredit on the single patriarchal figure, did not seem to work too well in the bipartite structure of leadership (initially with Bulganin, and later with Mikoyan). When he was deposed, his successors clearly indicated an intent to reinstitute the bipartite structure.

These few examples from the world of government and politics illustrate clearly the existence of different structures in power constellations. From observations of government, business, and other complex organizations several main types of constellation appear repeatedly. The types are distinguishable in how the members of the power constellation are situated around the central figure. There are four types seen frequently enough to warrant some analysis: (1) the patriarchy; (2) the group; (3) the triad; (4) the pair.

The Patriarchy

The patriarchy is the most traditional form of power structure. It involves a central figure who is powerful in the resources he commands, in his capacity to reward and punish, and in his personal magnetism or *charisma*. The subordinates working within the patriarchy stand equidistant from the central figure with the power of command clearly in his hands. He may be both revered and feared, and in the existence of these ambivalent feelings clearly attached to him lies a source of control. The individual member achieves personal security and salience through maintaining his attachment to the patriarch. The cohesion of his power constellation stems directly from the common attachment to the central figure.

In deriving security and salience from the bond with the patriarch, the member gives up considerable independence of thought and action. He may therefore become restless, establishing one of the inherent weaknesses in the patriarchy.

The capacity of the patriarch to function in making decisions results from his position in the communication network of the constellation. All lines of communication lead to and away from him. Having access to more information than any of his subordinates heightens the dependency upon him.

The patriarchal constellation is seen frequently in family enterprise and in the underdeveloped nations. The era of the "captains of industry" in late nineteenth-century U.S. history was notable for the presence of strong patriarchal types like Carnegie, Vanderbilt, and Rockefeller. With the emergence of publicly held corporations separating ownership and management, patriarchal management began to disappear.

Widespread corporate ownership reduced the opportunity for the patriarch since considerable power and control moved into the hands of the board of directors. The diffusion of power undermines the foundation upon which the patriarchal form rests, namely, the consolidation of communication, control, and resources for reward and punishment.

The visibility of the modern corporation also blocks the development of the patriarchy. Sewell Avery, of Montgomery Ward fame, may have been the last of the notorious patriarchs. His downfall began when the conflict with the U.S. government brought him out into the open in competition with figures more powerful than he. He was not only physically removed from office, even if only temporarily, but later abandoned by key executives who left Montgomery Ward en masse, because of disputes in policy and management. This public display of conflict and disagreement undermined the confidence of shareholders, further weakening Avery's position.

Another weakness in the patriarchal structure is encountered during management succession. Undoubtedly many patriarchs entertain the fantasy of their indestructability, a fantasy soon overtaken by the realities of physical disability and death.

In a small family corporation that I studied in the late 1940s, problems attendant to succession threatened the long-term stability of the organization. The corporation had been founded and managed successfully by a gifted inventor whose flair for technical innovation established his company in a specialized segment of the machine-tool industry. His son could not find a place for himself in the business and when the old gentleman died the presidency passed to a young grandson who had relatively little experience. The new president soon found himself in a rivalry with the head of sales who had worked closely with the company founder. The success of the young president hinged upon his capacity to establish authority in his position where he had none of the obvious qualities of his predecessor.

A similar transition faced young Henry Ford in taking over the Ford Motor Company upon his grandfather's death. In this case we could see the pivotal role played by the investment bankers and other outside board members in providing the transitional support until the new chief executive could consolidate the authority formerly vested in a patriarchal figure into his hands, although in modified form.

The Group

The group as a power constellation appears as an antithesis to the patriarchy. Here the members of the executive group stand as equals with no one person securing a favored position by virtue of the formal organization. Decision depends upon discussion and consensus with full airing of opinions preceding any intention to act. Once concensus is reached, group members are expected to implement the decision according to their division of responsibilities.

The cohesion of the group and its survival depends upon the commitment of members to a set of ideals. The ideals exist as the main source of authority in the group. The fact that ideals are not personified in any living member of the group, but instead may reside in the history of the organization, reduces ambivalent attitudes of members toward symbols of authority.

The group form of power constellation is found most frequently in nonprofit, philanthropic, and educational institutions. These institutions, more than business, articulate ideals that make it possible for members to attach themselves to a common frame of reference.

The ideals are at once a source of strength and weakness in the group structure. As abstract principles, ideals serve to guide strategy and tactics in the utilization of power. The group may function well insofar as the ideals are relevant to the current conditions and problems facing an organization. Any set of ideals, however, can introduce rigidities in defining the purposes of an organization and the paths of action needed to achieve goals.

The nature of these rigidities is clearly visible in the problems of Eastern European nations in their historical attachment to Marxism. The simple dichotomy of the Marxist revolution between capital and labor does not hold up in dealing with the realities of economic development, the pressure for higher standards of living, and the requirements of coexistence in avoiding the holocaust of nuclear war. We find, therefore, changes taking place in Hungary, Poland, and in the Soviet Union itself, calling for the adoption of economic approaches formerly identified with the capitalistic nations. Foremost among these changes is the increasing awareness that productivity requires competent professional management in socialist states no less than in capitalist states.

Another dilemma encountered in the group form of power constellation is the inhibition in decision making arising from simultaneously relying upon consensus while masking power differentials among members. Any decision involves the ascendance of certain themes over others. These themes are represented in the points of view held by group members. Should the organization undertake a new program, expand existing ones, or stand pat in the face of conditions in the environment? Answers to such policy questions do not emerge through espousing abstract ideals. In the course of finding answers, group members as policy makers take concrete positions and in effect play out the struggle for ascendancy. The unwillingness to engage in the struggle results in failure to decide and the ultimate stultification of the organization. The engagement of the issues, however, results in power differentials since some views will come to dominate others. In this way the ideal of equal distribution of power in the executive group breaks down and sows the seeds for a new type of power constellation.

The group form of power constellation arises sometimes as a result of abdication of responsibility. A chief executive who himself has many mixed feelings about the power invested in his position may seek to redistribute his influence and place it in the hands of a group of equals. This committee form of management soon breaks down because usually members are reluctant to assume the powers that are placed in their hands through uncertainty. The result is organizational paralysis.

As the group power constellation breaks down smaller coalitions emerge. These smaller subgroups may engage in rivalrous activity leading to domination by one of the coalitions. The next type of power constellation, the triad, represents a structure that can emerge from the dissolution of the group.

The Triad

Power constellations smaller than the group require a workable division of roles among members. This distribution must result in a specialization and complementation of the roles for the system to operate in a balanced way. Otherwise the power constellations that stand between the patriarchy and the group as extreme types could not function for long.

The triad as one such smaller unit consists of three figures, two of whom are subordinate to the central person. In business organizations the triad of president, executive vice president (for operations) and controller represents a typical arrangement. In such a triad, the president may concern himself with external affairs of the firm and emphasize marketing, purchasing and financing—all activities related to the "clients" of the organization. The executive vice president may deal with internal operations like manufacturing and research and development. The controller may specialize in information and feedback, activities that cut across both external and internal relations.

Besides specializing according to activities, following roughly the external-internal division, the members of the triad may play different kinds of expressive roles in the business. An expressive role refers to the total emotional qualities that dominate the way the person behaves within and outside the immediate power constellation. In the illustration just cited, the president may represent the impulsive, gregarious, optimistic and expansive figure, while the controller the withdrawn, pessimistic, conservative and withholding figure. In a balanced system of expressive roles, the executive vice president may represent the middle position between these two extremes. His behavior may reflect a steady responsive tone, warm without being exuberant, quizzical without being melancholy.

The triad, as other small power constellations, tends to take on symbolic significance that serves to represent the structure to the clients and members of the organization. In the above illustration the symbolization of the triad around impulse, restriction, and mediation is sufficiently familiar that it becomes easily recognized, although not necessarily conscious, to members and outsiders alike.

The symbolization of the triad as a power constellation may also be patterned along family lines, the most basic of all organizations. In a study recently completed, Richard Hodgson, Daniel Levinson, and I observed the work of the executive triad in an important teaching and research hospital.[2] The three men, all doctors who had gained recognition in their field, were in the key positions of superintendent, clinical director, and director of research. The superintendent occupied the position of "Number One" and specialized in external relations. The clinical director concentrated on patient care and residency training, and the director of research, as the title implies, was responsible for managing a large research program. These three task specializations did not mean that the three men restricted their activity. In a real sense, all three operated in one another's arena, yet each person had a delineated area of task specialization clearly visible to the entire organization.

The three members of this constellation were distinctly different in character structure and personality so that the family symbolization appeared strong in their interpersonal relations. The superintendent was an active, assertive, dominating, and forceful individual and appeared as a *paternal* figure in the organization. The clinical director was warm, quiet, giving, and appeared as a nurturant *maternal* figure. The director of research was egalitarian, permissive, almost boyish in his enthusiasm, and appeared similar to the *uncle* in many family structures.

These three emotional specializations complemented one another and further balanced the power constellation. There was no obvious competition among the three principals and the constellation had a degree of coherence easily represented to the organi-

[2] R. C. Hodgson, D. J. Levinson, and A. Zaleznik, *The Executive Role Constellation: An Analysis of Personality and Role Relations in Managment* (Boston, Division of Research, Harvard University Graduate School of Business Administration, 1965).

zation. But the very quality of family symbolization provided for certain rewards and costs that had to be assessed continually since there was always the danger that the costs would exceed the rewards and throw the system out of balance. This condition in fact occurred gradually and led to the dissolution of this constellation in favor of another structure.

This structure generated rewards and costs closely resembling the economy of a family. The "paternal" figure saw to it that people made decisions and saw them through. He contributed a sense of action and movement. But at the same time, more than a few subordinates feared him for his very qualities of assertiveness. They therefore avoided him and weakened his lines of communication throughout the organization. An individual cannot easily represent his organization to important outsiders if he feels he has lost touch with the thinking and activity of people within the organization. He needs a sense of confidence in the organizations' attachment to him as a figure and as a person.

The "maternal" figure reaped the rewards of close emotional ties to people in the organization and a sense of intimate knowledge of what went on in their daily work. The costs in his role, however, were substantial. He could not get his subordinates to face up to areas of weakness in performance and to change their behavior. Their attachment to him excluded evaluation since through selective perception they accepted only the nurturant aspects of the relationship and resisted the enforcement of standards. What subordinates accept and reject in a relationship has important effects on how a power figure consolidates his role. If he acts only on the gratifying elements of his role, he will soon become lopsided in his performance to the detriment of his own development and the organization's effectiveness.

The third figure, who symbolically functioned as the "uncle" in this power constellation, experienced the least stable position and ultimately left the organization. But while a member of the triad he organized a substantial research program, whose success depended on his ability to attract and encourage younger men to undertake studies. His egalitarian and permissive ways helped in reducing the formidable barriers to research that existed in the fantasies of younger men. These fantasies were built on the dichotomy of success and failure—the "all-or-nothing" approach. They will discover great things and become Nobel Laureates or fail dismally and live in obscurity. The truth of research in the image of the toilers in the vineyard—people working away day by day making small but, in the long run, important contributions—had to be communicated.

The permissive figure helped to bring this reality into the minds of would-be researchers and his rewards came through the accomplishment of work. But the costs of his obscurity in the triad and consequently the organization as a whole resulted in an unfavorable personal balance so that he chose to leave this organization.

Research studies as well as the lore of common sense suggest that triads are unstable structures. The danger that a pairing will emerge and exclude the third figure contributes to this instability. No matter what forces contribute to maintaining or dissolving the triad as a workable power constellation, it inevitably forces a comparison with the pair as an alternative coalition.

The Pair

In considering the pair as a power constellation, we can turn first to some mundane yet important laboratory studies of group behavior. Professor R. F. Bales, of the Department of Social Relations at Harvard University, studied the emergence of leadership structures in small groups organized to discuss human relations problems.[3] Trained observers recorded the behavior of participants and through the technique of the Post-Meeting Reaction Questionnaire collected data on role perceptions.

The data showed a tendency for the emergence of bipartite leadership in the groups. One individual assumed task leadership

[3] See Robert F. Bales, "The Equilibrium Problem in Small Groups," *Working Papers in the Theory of Action,* by T. Parsons, R. F. Bales, and E. A. Shils (Glencoe, Ill., Free Press, 1953).

and the second social leadership. The task leader actively oriented and moved the group in work performance while the social leader, through a passive style, provided for tension reduction and group cohesion. Bales's findings suggested that effective group performance depended on cooperation between the task and social leader. This coalition in the form of the pair, obviously, followed the lines of the paternal-maternal unit in the family.

The relevance of the pair as a power constellation goes beyond the laboratory. In observing an executive organization in a growing and successful company, my colleagues and I found the relationship between the president and vice president patterned like the pairing in the family. The president, an aggressive assertive man, assumed leadership in the strategy and tactics of product development. The company had successfully diversified and converted itself from a producer of consumer products into an industrial complex utilizing a sophisticated technology.

The vice president, a passive man, specialized in internal management. He served as the conservative force in the organization who modified the impact of the forceful president on subordinates.

As in all power constellations, the pair operates on a balance of rewards and costs both for individuals and for the organization. In the case just cited, the costs of the pairing were beginning to be felt in the inability of this organization to hold bright and ambitious young men with specialized education in the company's newer technical fields. The internal management of the firm centered in the social leader who resisted change in the introduction of new people and new modes of operation. Presumably organization change in this situation depended upon a prior shift in the executive power constellation, a step neither principal in the pair seemed able to take.

THE DYNAMICS OF POWER CONSTELLATIONS

Resistance to change as a consequence of the balance of forces within a power constellation brings us to the question of the underlying dynamics of these executive structures. Power constellations form and persist because of their relevance to the motivations of the principals and the needs of the organization. In understanding the motivational side of power constellations I shall present a case study taken from the literature in political science. The interpretation will utilize concepts from psychoanalytic psychology, particularly those ideas that help us to understand the impact of unconscious processes on personality and action.

Woodrow Wilson and Colonel House: A Case Study

Alexander and Juliette George published an historical study of the administrative relationship between Woodrow Wilson and Colonel House, who formed a power constellation along the lines of the pair structure.[4] The unique feature of this study is in the authors' attempt to use personality theory in interpreting the process of leadership. While much of what the Georges did in their study is open to question, as to both the adequacy in the data they utilize and the salience of their psychological interpretations, nevertheless the study makes a remarkable contribution to the understanding of the human aspects of leadership. At any rate, it provides us with an intriguing example of the motivations that sustain and then lead to the demise of a two-person power constellation.

I should emphasize at the outset that the purpose in studying motivation, leadership, and interpersonal relations is to illuminate the ways in which power is consolidated and used in formulating decisions. It is not to assert the naïve position that personality determines history—that, for example, the United States failed to

---

[4] Alexander and Juliette L. George, *Woodrow Wilson and Colonel House, A Personality Study* (New York: Dover Publications, 1964).

enter the League of Nations simply because Wilson's neurotic conflicts affected his approach to the United States Senate. The Georges are quite clear on this point. Their aim is to explain a recurrent theme in Wilson's pattern of leadership: his inability to deal flexibly with conflicts of position and to negotiate for solutions. In two instances in his career, Wilson entered into a struggle over policy and was defeated. The first instance occurred during the latter years of his presidency at Princeton University; the second during his struggle over the peace treaty and the entry of the United States into the League of Nations.

The main explanatory theme in the Georges' interpretation is that Wilson's failure to act flexibly stemmed from aggressive impulses that were repressed or buried in his personality organization. Wilson was an idealist and acted most comfortably as the orator, appealing to the public around the grand visions of peace, democracy, and reform. He had a distaste for the processes of negotiation and encountered difficulties with the Congress, the representatives of the allies in Paris, and earlier in his career with the faculty and trustees of Princeton.

The Georges suggest by way of further explanation that Wilson's repressed aggression related to unconscious hostility toward his father. Wilson maintained markedly ambivalent attitudes toward his father, who was an exacting and stern man, not reluctant to use humiliation in his influence over his son during the important formative years. Wilson openly adored his father and could not accept consciously the possibility of aggression toward this beloved figure in his life. The hostility remained unconscious subject to the defenses of repression and reaction formation. Reaction formation in his defense against anxiety stemming from unacceptable impulses consisted of idealizing the relationship in a way that masked the opposite feelings of anger and hostility. It followed the pattern of converting hate into love to avoid conflict and anxiety that arise in the recognition of one's total attitude toward an important figure like a parent.

That idealization played an important part in Wilson's character structure is illustrated in the following letter the young man wrote to his father during a separation at the Christmas season. The Georges quote the letter written when Wilson was a young adult recently married.

My precious father,

My thoughts are full of you and dear "Dode"* all the time. Tennessee seems so far away for a chap as hungry as I am for a sight of the two men whom I love. As the Christmas recess approaches I realize, as I have so often before, the pain there is in a season of holiday and rejoicing away from you. As you know, one of the chief things about which I feel most warranted in rejoicing is that I am your son. I realize the benefit of being your son more and more as my talents and experience grow; I recognize the strength growing in me as of the nature of your strength; I become more and more conscious of the hereditary wealth I possess; that capital of principle, of literary force and skill, of capacity for firsthand thought; and I feel daily more and more bent toward creating in my own children that combined respect and tender devotion for their father that you gave your children for you. Oh, how happy I should be, if I could make them think of me as I think of you! You have given me a love that grows, that is stronger in me now that I am a man than it was when I was a boy, and which will be stronger in me when I am an old man than it is now—a love, in brief, that is rooted and grounded in reason, and not in filial instinct merely—a love resting upon abiding foundations of service, recognizing you as in a certain real sense the author of all I have to be so grateful for! I bless God for my noble, strong, and saintly mother and for my incomparable father. Ask "Dode" if he does not subscribe? and tell him that I love my brother passionately.

. . . Ellie joins me in unbounded love to you both.

Your devoted son,
Woodrow[5]

One must be struck, along with the authors of this study, with the effusiveness of this letter to Wilson's father, a quality suggestive of idealization and reaction formation. But equally suggestive and of great potential importance in the study of Wilson as a

* Wilson's younger brother Joseph.
[5] *Ibid.*, p. 10.

leader is the reference to his brother. Wilson innocently asks for the comparison between himself and his brother in their love for their father. The brother could scarcely be more eloquent in his expression of love. The theme is therefore broadened to one of sibling rivalry and the related disappointments in love and rivalry, issues largely overlooked in the Georges' interpretive framework.

The sibling rivalry must be taken into account in developing the relationship between Wilson's conflicts and his work as a leader. His difficulties at Princeton centered largely in his disagreements with the dean of the Graduate School. Wilson's behavior during the episode of the formation of the Graduate School appeared markedly inconsistent, rigid, and at times irrational—the type of behavior suggestive of the eruption of internal conflict into external behavior.

Wilson's relationship to House and the mutual pattern of influence between these two brilliant men can be explored in this same context. While Wilson was idealistic and exhibitionistic in his behavior as a leader, House was the realist. He preferred to work behind the scenes and to negotiate with an appreciation for the necessary details in the process of negotiation. He seemed to adore Wilson and was as effusive in his praise of Wilson as the latter had been toward his own father. Aggression was no problem in this relationship so long as the two men complemented each other with a pattern of Wilson as the adored, and House as the adoring figure. Within this relationship both men were extremely forceful and had considerable influence on events.

The two men first met while Wilson was Governor of New Jersey. House, who was accustomed to "behind the scenes" action in political affairs and the role of "king maker," found in Wilson an ideal candidate for the Presidency on the Democratic ticket. House contributed considerably to Wilson's success at the Democratic Convention and his later campaign. During Wilson's first term and for much of his second term, House acted as his most trusted adviser and wielded enormous influence on decisions, particularly those affecting appointments. The basic change in this relationship between the two men involved a shift in the balance between activity and passivity in their interactions. Instead of indirect and manipulative influence attempts using flattery and acquiescence, House became more openly critical of Wilson's ability to negotiate and formulate workable compromises.

This shift in the relationship coincided also with Wilson's second marriage. According to the evidence presented by the Georges, the second Mrs. Wilson developed an almost intuitive dislike for House, suggestive of rivalry between the two for influence and affection in the eyes of Wilson. The first Mrs. Wilson appeared to achieve her gratifications through adoration of her husband. What seemed gratifying for him received her support. In this vein, Wilson's relationship to House received her unfailing support and did not entail rivalry for attention. The situation changed with the second marriage. The second Mrs. Wilson appeared more active and aggressive than the first, and she viewed House with sufficient suspicion to suggest that he aroused important conflicts for her. Just what these conflicts were remains unclear in this study.

We therefore find as one important theme for further understanding the dynamics of the power constellations, the development of an interpersonal structure whose meaning in the unconscious of the actors assumes prime significance in understanding the playout of personal conflicts, especially as these conflicts affect perception, thinking, and decision making within an administrative context.

The main elements to be explored in these structures are first, how the past tends to be recreated in the present in the sense in which the persons in the structure take on meaning as objects of love and hate from early family history. This element is recognizable as the transference reactions in everyday life—"transference" referring to the carryover of intense feelings from the past into the present. These transference reactions are recognizable in the sense that in observing behavior of executives, one would face great difficulty in finding explanations for the intense emotional reactions individuals experience in their human relationships in work settings without the idea that individuals frequently relive the unsolved problems from their personal history in their present relationships.

In Wilson's case, one could speculate that his relationship to House had intense emotional and symbolic meaning in at least three senses: First, as a representation of a sibling relationship in which the two "brothers" worked as allies, instead of rivals for the affection and esteem of powerful and loved parents. The alliance served to foster cooperation instead of competition. Second, as a relationship between father and son where through identification with the father Wilson assumed the position of both loved and feared parent. While identifying with and re-enacting his father's role Wilson also could relive the position of the adoring son in the type of attachment he established with House. In this re-enactment of both the adoring and the adored figures, within this single interpersonal structure, Wilson could realize both the satisfactions of another person's adoration and also the defense against anxiety that could be maintained in the idealization that was such an integral part of the relationship.

The third way of understanding the symbolic significance of the relationship is in the re-enactment of the role of father and mother in the pair relationship. Here again, identification plays an important part in understanding the dynamic meaning of the structure. In this case, I would speculate that through the distribution of active and passive modes of behavior within the pairing, the relationship tended to connect with earlier fantasies of the relationships between the parents.

In turning the pair structure around, from the vantage point of House, one is equally struck by the effects of reproducing the past in the present. While the data were limited, the repetition elements appeared through the connection between House's earlier relationships with an older brother and his preferred style of work. House had an older brother, James, to whom he felt deeply attached. In fact, the family referred to the younger boy as the "second Jimmie" in recognition of their closeness. James was killed in an accident—he fell from a trapeze and died of a brain injury when the younger House was ten years old. Two years later, House had an incredibly similar accident and, while he recovered, he was no longer physically robust. His pattern of activity and aspirations changed markedly following this accident.

While the authors themselves make no interpretations of these events and relationships, the implication is quite clear that House's relationship with his brother carried many fantasies involving active-passive, and leader-follower, components. It seems very likely that House was reliving, in part at least, his past relationship to the older brother through the pair structure he created with Woodrow Wilson.

Another element in the attempt to interpret the significance of the interpersonal structures in work settings is the dynamics of gratification and defense, which again can be seen in their development through understanding of the past. We have already seen the suggestion that in the pairing relationship active and passive wishes can be gratified, although in highly disguised form. Similarly, the relationship can contain and manage the strong aggressive impulses which for an individual such as Wilson can be highly problematic and a source of anxiety.

Wilson was at his best when the injustices of the world and the defects in government could be the objects of his attacks. If at the same time the interpersonal relationships he created and experienced served to reinforce the view that he was a constructive and loving man, then his own aggressive wishes toward significant objects of the past were safely buried.

Still a third element in this problem is to discover the adaptive features of these interpersonal structures in permitting a style of work that often proves highly effective. There is little question, for example, that Wilson and House had created an effective pairing to accomplish much important work. There existed in their differentiation of role, with the particular emotional qualities implied in this division of effort, a useful leadership structure and apparatus for making decisions. Its adaptive values centered around the division between idealism and realism. Wilson the orator could inspire and move men's minds around important national and human aspirations. House the negotiator could strive for the agreements and compromises so necessary in arriving at decisions that work because they reflect consensus over desirable goals. As long as this division of function served to gratify the wishes of the individuals, the relationship remained intact and functioned well. When the balance began to shift with new emotional investments the relationship lost its capacity to bind dynamic conflicts significant in the development of each of these two men.

In presenting material from the history of the administrative relationship between Wilson and House I have tried to illustrate the types of material and explanations that are intrinsic to the study of power constellations. The materials consist of emotional, behavioral, and cognitive content of management. The explanations depend upon the examination of symbolic aspects of interpersonal relations and their connections with the dynamics of executive motivation. Here the relationship between individual history and unconscious conflicts acted out in the present is by no means limited to the study of governmental power constellations. This approach to power constellations applies equally well to all formal organizations, including business. It may be useful at this point to return to illustrations drawn directly from industrial organizations.

The Dynamics of the Pairing in Industrial Organizations

In the illustration I presented earlier of the pair relationship in a growing business, I outlined the way the president and vice president worked in their power constellation. This power constellation functioned as much on the emotional specializations of the two executives as on their division of formal responsibility. The symbolism of an aggressive, assertive man paired with a passive, nurturant man re-created the classical parental situation in the family. This symbolism served as an anchor point to which each principal in the pair could play out his personal conflicts by re-creating the past in the present. It also served as an anchor point that oriented subordinates to an internally evolving executive structure.

The structure had both positive and negative effects on the work of the organization. The positive effects consisted of the softening of the impact of aggression on the emotional economy of subordinates while permitting rapid innovations in work. The negative effects consisted of resistance to change through conservative attachments between subordinates and the "maternal-like" vice president.

In a pair relationship, such as this one, the anxiety provoking acts and the avoidances of one actor are precisely the adaptive features of the behavior of the second actor. In this sense, the pair is complementary and probably effects important outcomes for work and problem solving. The difficulty in such pair relationships, however, is in their potential for resistance to change both within the individuals concerned and in the organization.

In the industrial company in our illustration, the president of necessity recruited new types of professional research workers, engineers, and managers following the introduction of product innovation. These men, some of whom had Ph.D.s in special fields thought and communicated in symbol systems foreign to the traditions of the organization, traditions supported and reinforced by the vice president.

In following the history of the organization over several years, we found a markedly high turnover rate among the new professionals. I would attribute the inability to hold these very competent men to the resistance to change imbedded in the unconscious meaning of this pair relationship. The meaning related to a traditional identity of the organization that was hostile to the new identity of a technologically sophisticated organization. While holding to the old power constellation of the pair, the organization cast out the new breed of professionals, scientists, and technicians. In this sense, the stable interpersonal structure of the executive pair that served to permit actions and avoidances relavant to the developmental and motivational dynamics of the actors also become maladaptive in terms of the conscious goals of the leaders of the organization.

Maladaptive features of these interpersonal power constellations exist also in the continuing development of the individuals concerned. If we can refer back for a moment to the case of Wilson and House, I can illustrate this last point.

The fact that the relationship became so highly invested and represented deeply rooted wishes created sources of tension. House, it was clear, sought to change his relationship to Wilson to become the dominant-active partner in this pair, a reversal that was intolerable to Wilson. One could speculate on how Wilson's second marriage and the shift this meant in the individual's emotional investments contributed to the press for change.

We could equally consider the idea that individuals who attempt abruptly to shift their relationships and preferred work styles have experienced a form of behavior that involves the breakthrough of unconscious conflicts formerly buried and repressed. In any case, it is usually extremely difficult to alter these relationships to achieve a new balance, with the consequence that either the structure breaks down or returns to its prior state.

CONCLUSION

This analysis of power constellations in organizations affords a view of executive behavior. It stresses the motivational, emotional, and symbolic aspects of management and their relation to styles of work and effectiveness, both individual and organizational.

In outlining various types of power constellations and their dynamics I have merely suggested the form and content of a line of investigation in organization studies that has only really begun. This line of investigation draws together the understanding of how and why men work at the sources of power in organizations with the situational realities confronting these men. The encounter between man and situation is a process that can be understood and even managed by individuals who care to take the trouble to look at themselves as vital participants in the action of organizations.

The themes that go into the quality of this participation have been suggested in the material of this chapter. One crucial theme is the nature of executive styles of performance within power constellations. The next chapter turns more direct attention to these styles in the study of executive behavior and interpersonal competence.

9 / Interpersonal Competence in Management*

One of the questions that continues to intrigue active executives, as well as the social scientists who study their behavior, is how to account for the differences in the styles of behavior of managers. Commonsense observation indicates that the styles of behavior, including interpersonal relations, are just as varied among executives as among individuals in other professions. How do these different interpersonal styles relate to the way individuals pursue their careers? Is a given style to be considered superior to others? If so, by what criteria are such evaluations to be made? Can we demonstrate, for example, that a given style of behavior is tied to greater organizational effectiveness? Or is it possible that how an executive behaves in relation to other persons has less direct significance in organization outcomes than one might suppose at first glance?

The strength of the interest in the interpersonal relations of the executive is clearly indicated in the prevalence of human relations training programs. One of the stated aims in most of these programs is to improve the way executives behave in relation to their bosses, subordinates, and peers. The guidelines for changes in behavior seem to rest on a set of ideals as to what makes for

* Adapted from the article "Managerial Behavior and Interpersonal Competence" in the April 1964 issue of *Behavioral Science* © 1964 by Mental Health Research Institute, reprinted by permission.

competence in interpersonal behavior. Yet these ideals rest on a flimsy foundation of beliefs about how people should act and often ignore the deeper significance of action in terms of the development of the individual.

My main purpose in this chapter is to examine the adequacy of existing notions about interpersonal competence and its relation to the manager's job. A second purpose is to consider the best means by which any person's relationship with others may be improved. I intend in this discussion to raise critical questions about ideas that seem to be accepted as hard fact rather than simply as a philosophy and set of ideals for generating investigation.

EXECUTIVE FUNCTIONS

Managers work intensively in a structure of human relationships in which patterns of influence have important effects on results. Organizations are essentially systems of relationships in which individuals are bound together by purposes, ideologies, and expectations. These binding qualities identify the organization to those who participate in it or are its clients.

A manager in an organization, according to Chester Barnard, operates in two spheres simultaneously. He performs a set of functions that relate directly to the technical aspects of his job, such as deciding on a brand name for a new product or preparing a capital expenditures budget for the firm. Barnard calls these functions nonexecutive, and they can be expected to vary in content from job to job and organization to organization. Another set of functions that Barnard calls the executive functions of the manager deal with the organization as a cooperative system in which interpersonal relations are a significant aspect. To quote Barnard:

It is important to observe, however, that not all work done by persons who occupy executive positions is in connection with the executive functions, the coordination of activities of others. Some of the work of such persons, though *organization* work, is not executive. For example, if the president of a corporation goes out personally to sell products of his company or engages in some of the production work, these are not executive services. If the president of a university gives lectures to a class of students, this is not executive work. If the head of a government department spends time on complaints or disputes about services rendered by the department, this is not necessarily executive work. Executive work is not that *of* the organization, but the specialized work of *maintaining* the organization in operation.[1]

Earlier, Barnard states:

Organization results from the modification of the action of the individual through control of or influence upon . . . [(1) purposes, desires, impulses of the moment and, (2) the alternatives external to the individuals recognized by him as available]. Deliberate conscious and specialized control of them is the essence of the executive functions.[2]

Maintaining the Steady State

Barnard's ideas about executive functions illustrated in these two quotations serve to raise a fundamental issue on the nature of interpersonal competence in executive performance. Barnard stresses as the core of the executive function the problems arising from personal and interpersonal attributes of organizations as systems of cooperation. With his emphasis on executive work as "the specialized work of *maintaining* the organization," he implicitly points to interpersonal behavior of the executive that is directed toward assuring the internal stability of the organization. This function may properly be related to the process known in biology as "homeostasis." Walter Cannon discussed homeostasis as a quality of organisms that enables them to maintain a steady state in the face of changing conditions in the environment.[3] Usually this steady state is achieved through automatic

[1] C. Barnard, *The Functions of the Executive* (Cambridge: Harvard University Press, 1958), p. 215.
[2] *Ibid.*, p. 17.
[3] W. B. Cannon, *Bodily Changes in Pain, Hunger, Fear and Rage* (New York: D. Appleton and Company, 1915). W. B. Cannon, *The Way of an Investigator* (New York: W. W. Norton and Company, 1945).

controls that act as feedback and regulating devices.

Following this line of thought, one's attention is then directed toward an understanding of the interpersonal processes in organizations that are associated with maintaining balance and the steady state. I refer to these interpersonal processes as the *homeostatic* functions of the executive.

Mediating Relations with the Environment

The second part of the quotation from Barnard suggests another type of executive function, different from the need to maintain balanced relationships within the organization. Barnard indicated also that "organization results from the modification of the action of the individual through control and influence." This statement suggests, in other words, that the executive function proceeds through a kind of intervention, not directed necessarily toward maintaining a steady state, but directed instead toward altering behavior and attitudes with conscious intent. The direction the executive takes in his efforts to alter behavior is presumably determined by the organization's problems of living and surviving in its competitive environment. The environment with its social, political, and economic forces establishes a press on the organization that demands some internal change. The executive function in this case is to influence individuals and groups within the organization to modify behavior and attitudes so that it establishes some different relationship to environment.

To distinguish this second set of executive functions from "homeostasis" the term "mediative" seems appropriate since it refers to the internal changes in response to environmental pressures. Now presumably mediative functions imply certain kinds of interpersonal processes that may or may not be different from those established in connection with the problems of maintaining the steady state. I shall return to this issue later in the chapter because my objective is to analyze the different interpersonal processes with which managerial behavior is concerned and to reexamine competence in terms of the *multiple* functions of the executive rather than a single function that dictates a rather limited kind of interpersonal activity.

Proaction as an Executive Function

There is a third kind of executive function that is not clearly defined or understood by most students of organizations. If I were to try to establish a continuum along which to describe executive functions, particularly one that clarifies the different styles of interpersonal behavior, I would turn to the polar extremes of the passive-active forms of behavior.

The homeostatic functions of the executive are positioned toward the passive end of this scale since they serve the aims of balance and stability within the organization. The way the steady state is maintained would seem to depend upon a style of interpersonal behavior where the executive intervenes least. He uses instead the existing forces within the organization to permit the modest alterations necessary to return to the steady state. The problem is comparable to the healing process in medicine which adopts a conservative point of view concerning the role of the physician. This view, stated very clearly by Walter Cannon, is worth quoting. Cannon said, in his book, *The Wisdom of the Body:*

The fathers of medicine made use of the expression, "the healing force of nature." . . . it indicates, of course, recognition of the fact that processes of repair after injury, and restoration of health after disease go on quite independent of any treatment which a physician may give.[4]

Earlier, Cannon stated:

The ability of living beings to maintain their own constancy has long impressed biologists. The idea that disease is cured by natural processes . . . an idea which was held by Hippocrates (460-377 B.C.)

[4] W. B. Cannon, *The Wisdom of the Body* (New York: W. W. Norton and Company, 1932, p. 240.

implies the existence of agencies which are ready to operate correctively when the normal state of the organism is upset.[5]

If only by analogy, we can visualize the homeostatic functions as requiring very modest activity on the part of the executive to set in motion forces already existing within the organization to re-establish the steady state.

While space does not permit detailed illustrations, it would be worthwhile to note the types of situations that involve homeostatic processes in organizations. A good instance would be one where an internal disruption such as vying for informal leadership takes place in the otherwise cooperative relations among a group of employees. Such a disruption can occur at any level in the organization and requires the introduction of a corrective procedure. This procedure often consists of listening to the complaints of involved persons and helping them to assess reality. Such executive behavior is designed to reduce conflict and to restore prior conditions of balance. As such, it usually entails nondirective, passive behavior. Students of this process frequently draw on the analogy of individual psychotherapy to help describe the kind of behavior involved in these homeostatic functions. In psychotherapy, the burden of the "cure" is on the client. The counselor through passive listening and reflection helps the client to assess himself and his situation in more accurate terms.

The mediative functions are more active in character than those addressed to discharging tensions and restoring harmony. The primary difference arises from the source of stimulus for executive action. Mediative processes occur under the impact of environmental pressures. A set of forces in the environment creates the need for internal adaptation. As indicated earlier, the homeostatic functions become necessary where internal disruptions act as stimuli.

Mediative functions require a more active mode of behavior since they tap into functions that *only* managers can perform. Because of their location in the organization, managers stand

[5] *Ibid.*, pp. 20-21.

closer to the environment than do other employees, and the higher the manager's status, the more he becomes concerned with issues arising outside the boundaries of the firm.

In response to environmental pressures, the manager activates change. He formulates goals and communicates them within the internal network of the organization. Comparing the mediative with the homeostatic functions, the mode of interpersonal behavior tends to be more aggressive and less permissive. Nevertheless, the aggressive mode has certain limits in mediative functions. When it is possible, for example, to separate goals and objectives from means and procedures, managers may seek to limit aggressive responses to the formulation and communication of goals while withdrawing in favor of informal approaches for establishing means and procedures. This pattern is best illustrated under conditions of decentralization in an organization.

It would be grossly inadequate to restrict executive behavior to the homesostatic and mediative functions. Ordinary observation shows a type of executive function that actively seeks out environmental possibilities. Instead of being reactive to environmental pressures, the behavior is *proactive* and in a sense induces change in the environment to conform to the creative uses of resources available within the organization. The automobile, for example, was not produced because of environmental pressures, but rather from innovative behaviors of certain individuals, who applied a new level of technological sophistication to transportation. For purposes of discussion, I have called this third set of executive functions the proactive, although innovative would do just as well.

On the whole, we know little about the psychology of innovation, particularly in the nature of human relations that affect innovation. But what we do know suggests that individuals convert and release aggressive energy generated within themselves, but directed outward toward changing the environment. Innovation is anything but conservative, and typically because of its use of aggression may result in resistance, counteraggression, and in some cases outright hostility.

There are other important differences in comparing proactive with the more conservative homeostatic and mediative functions. In terms of the selection of goals, the executive concerned with homeostasis usually ends up stressing the desirability of balance and harmony, sometimes to the point where it becomes, inadvertently perhaps, a substitute for activity on the environment. Proaction, at the other extreme, actually disrupts internal relations in the interests of changing the environment.

The three types of executive functions demand different styles of interpersonal behavior, thinking, and problem solving. Just how these differences become manifest in organizations and with what consequences requires far more research than has been done to date. But, it is clear that any consideration of interpersonal competence has to center on just what executive functions the competence is directed toward. I shall return to this issue later in the chapter. In the meantime, I should like to shift the course of this discussion from the description of executive functions to an explanation of their implementation in managerial behavior.

Executive Behavior and Personality Dynamics

The psychoanalytic study of personality and character (as developed by Sigmund Freud) provides potentially the fullest and most challenging statement of the conditions in human development that determine the way executives pattern their role.

The three types of executive functions provide the nucleus of a description of the executive role. But the full performance of the role is styled according to the dynamic trends in personality. The trends that seem especially important for the question of interpersonal competence relate to the structure and function of the ego.

The concept of the ego refers to the management apparatus within the personality—the apparatus that regulates the exchange between the inner and outer worlds of the individual. The quality and style of ego functions of the adult is an outcome of development during the formative years. Included in development are the biological functions that proceed according to a timetable in which tensions and gratifications center around shifting body zones and exchanges with the mother and later the father in the family circle.

As the individual matures and masters the conflicts between biological tensions and the realities of human existence, the qualities of personality take form and substance. These qualities then enter into the later life tasks of development and account for the relative degrees of success or failure in maturation.

One of the most common sources of confusion in the minds of many people concerning Freud's theory of human development is the belief that Freud viewed development as effectively concluded and sealed off by the time the individual experienced the Oedipus complex and entered the latency period (approximately age six). This erroneous belief probably exists because emphasis is in fact given to the early stages of childhood as major building-blocks of later development. Freud did not, however, suggest that developmental processes in later life stages are irrelevant. Rather, he established the crucial role of the formative years and part of the unfinished business in developmental theory is to establish the connections among all the stages of the life cycle, including the career years.

Patterns of Emotional Investment in Career

In considering the issues of interpersonal competence in the managerial role, we are faced immediately with problems of understanding development in the career years in relation to both earlier and later stages in the life cycle. By the time an individual reaches an organization to embark on a managerial career, he has established internal predispositions of personality that characterize how he seeks to engage his environment. The predispositions represent in part the distribution of emotional investments or energy.

The objects toward which energy can be directed are other

persons or ideas and thought patterns. To illustrate this division of emotional investment, I can cite some evidence from the study of career patterns of managers and scientists.

Colleagues and I studied career patterns among a group of professional employees who worked in a research and development laboratory.[6] Some of these employees expressed the intention to follow a specialist career route in which their main interest was in technical work. Others expressed an intention to assume a management job.

All of the employees wrote a series of imaginative stories in response to ambiguous pictures. This procedure, known as a projective test, is based on the idea that the stimulus can provoke a wide range of responses depending upon the concerns of the subjects as reflected in their inner fantasy and thought processes. The particular pictures, part of the series in Murray's Thematic Apperception Test,[7] seemed suitable for a fairly wide range of fantasy productions. Two of them showed a single individual in an otherwise unpopulated scene.

As one might expect, the stories written in response to these two pictures showed interesting differences in the concerns of the managerial and technical types of individuals. The would-be managers wrote stories in which they populated the themes with individuals in interaction. The technical types wrote stories in which the individual in the picture, the "hero," was in the midst of thought or solitary activity without the direct presence of other persons.

I think we can assume that the extent to which an individual's fantasy productions create an interpersonal or solitary world reflect his emotional investments as well as preferred style of work. Other investigations along similar lines separate the person-oriented from the idea-oriented individual and the "introverted" from the "extroverted" personality.

The division between person-oriented and idea-oriented is,

[6] A. Zaleznik, G. Dalton, L. B. Barnes, *Orientation and Conflict in Career*, (manuscript to be published by the Division of Research, Harvard Graduate School of Business Administration).

[7] H. A. Murray, *et al.*, *Explorations in Personality* (New York: Oxford University Press, 1938).

however, an oversimplified view of the distribution of emotional investments among individuals in work organizations. For purposes of further analysis, let us examine three basic patterns: (1) the person-oriented; (2) the idea- or task-oriented; and (3) the fusion-oriented.

1. *The Person-Oriented:* The person-oriented individual invests energy in relationships with other persons. Tasks or ideas have little relevance as entities of thought and work. Instead, being with and acting through other persons represent the "natural" state of affairs. Usually a strongly person-oriented individual may be unaware or unreceptive to the demands of solitary activity, achievement, and technical competence.

The strong features of the ego of the person-oriented individual are in his tolerance of intimacy in human relationships. The acceptance of feelings and expression of warmth and caring reflect the tendency to depend upon others in the control of work in organizations.

The style of behavior leans toward passivity and incorporation. The person-oriented individual absorbs from others and, therefore, permits the expression of feelings, particularly those related to affection and intimacy.

There are weaknesses of the ego that also enter into the transactions preferred by the person-oriented individual. The weakness appears at the extremes of the types, but also reflects underlying personality trends in individuals who invest their energy mainly in human relationships. These individuals may be excessively dependent upon others and unable to tolerate aggression either in themselves or in other persons. The preferred relationships are lateral, peerlike, and friendly.

In studying a sample of the fantasy productions of a group of person-oriented individuals, the nature of preferred relationships were woven into story themes in response to an ambiguous picture showing two males standing side by side in a rural setting.[8] The person-oriented individuals wrote stories inventing a

---

[8] D. Moment, and A. Zaleznik, *Role Development and Interpersonal Competence* (Cambridge: Division of Research, Harvard Graduate School of Business Administration, 1963).

friendly relationship between the men who were cast as either longstanding friends or as uncle and nephew. A vertical authority relationship was notable for its absence along with themes of disagreement and competition.

Extreme cases of investment in persons may reflect, besides a low tolerance for aggression in self and others, a relatively lowered sense of self-confidence. Affirmation of self may be sought through acceptance by others. Conformity and conservatism may therefore exist as strong trends in the work and thought styles of person-oriented individuals.

2. *The Idea- or Task-Oriented:* Individuals who are oriented toward ideas or tasks in their preferred approach to work appear opposite to the person-oriented in the many ways one can describe styles of work. Individuals of this type engage in and derive rewards from task accomplishment rather than friendship and approval from others. The intrinsic challenges of technical work, whether in manipulation of abstract ideas or "hardware," engage interests and attention. People are acknowledged and engaged, but at the level of task-directed activity rather than personality and feelings. The more tender side of human relationships are reserved for the family so that idea-oriented individuals make a sharp separation between work and home. They react to these settings in different ways and expect different things from each.

The main ego strengths of idea-oriented individuals relate to work performance. Through emphasis on tangible productivity, idea men have a strong basis for achievement and gratification that may offset their limited rewards of warmth and friendship from work associates. They experience little anxiety over the display of aggression and indeed activate aggression in others through vigorous and energetic displays of effort. To generate aggression around work means it is necessary to tolerate aggression from within as well as from without. Here task-oriented people seem to excel in their readiness to engage the world of work and persons in competitive relationships.

The ego weaknesses of this type center around the need to

defend themselves against displays of intimacy in others and deeply rooted passive wishes that occasionally emerge from the depths of their own personality. The ambiguity of human emotions arouses concern, particularly in the problem of achieving comradeship and the appropriate degree of closeness with their male associates.

In the illustration from fantasy projections of preferred work relationships of the person-oriented types, I indicated the marked inclination for friendly and egalitarian attitudes. The idea-oriented seem to prefer vertical relationships of authority and express themes involving competition and aggression. This preferred work structure seems consistent with individuals whose main concerns relate to achievement and mastery rather than warmth and intimacy. It is not that idea-oriented types are hostile to people; rather, they bring considerable aggressive energies to bear on their work. It is as though the supremacy of the task objectives blunt consideration for feelings rather than express directly hostile intentions toward other persons. Needless to say, especially sensitive individuals who are unable to cope with aggression have difficulty getting on with task-oriented individuals.

3. *The Fusion-Oriented:* Persons with a third type of orientation that seems to stand apart from either the extremes of person and idea types invest emotional energy in a fusion of objects. Work is conceived of as a process that has neither a discrete beginning nor a definitive end. The process consists of the exchange and integration of ideas through human communications.

Fusion types may be concerned with achievement, but relate outcomes to organized human effort. This type is highly concerned with organizations and the structure in which work proceeds.

Fusion-oriented persons can accept both intimacy and aggression, but seek to channel energies toward the procedures and flow of work. They generally accept the vertical nature of authority and are willing to attempt to influence others at the level of ideas or procedures for communication. They also accept aggres-

sion and competition from others and seem on the whole to neu-
tralize the competition so that inanimate objects are under attack
rather than persons.

The ego strengths of fusion types are considerable, including
capacity to wait and work for gratifications. Their view is long-
range combined with a sensitivity to action and interaction in the
here and now.

Studies of the fusion types suggest they are vulnerable to anxiety over their responsibilities. Failure to meet responsibilities and
obligations to others results in a sense of dread. To be at odds
with society as represented by work associates and family is extremely painful even in fantasy. This avoidance of super-ego
guilt is a strong motivator to assume responsible and socially
acceptable attitudes. The result is often conformity in action and
conventionality in thinking.

In the study of fantasy productions of the fusion-oriented type
of person, I have found ample evidence of ideas suggestive of
clichés. As long as the individuals exist in a close degree of harmony with their social environment, there seems to be little need
to stretch beyond the accepted tensions of life and the conventional modes of resolution. As a result, the fusion-oriented type
may not experience himself very deeply. This almost superficial
sense of self leads to a kind of optimistic representation to others
that dampens the degree of conflict others experience when
working with the fusion types. It also, however, tends to dampen
the degree of creativity in work.

The fusion types as observed in work and experimental settings
suggest by analogy the description in William James's *Varieties
of Religious Experience* of the "once-born" personality. James
states,

In many persons, happiness is congenital and irreclaimable.
"Cosmic emotion" inevitably takes in them the form of enthusiasm
and freedom. I speak not only of those who are animally happy. I
mean those who, when unhappiness is offered or proposed to them,
positively refuse to feel it, as if it were something mean and wrong.
We find such persons in every age, passionately flinging themselves

upon their sense of goodness of life, in spite of the hardships of their own condition, and in spite of the sinister theologies into which they may be born.[9]

The portrayal of fusion types as optimistic and in harmony with their environment suggests both the strengths and the weaknesses in their approach to work. The strengths lie in energetic work that takes account of persons, and the weaknesses lie in the conventional approach that can at times border on superficiality.

Here, as with all styles of work, we cannot view the strengths and weaknesses of the individual except in relation to the slow but deep-seated development of the individual's ego. The nature of this development points to the relatively limited capacity individuals have in making substantial alterations in their basic style. It would be worthwhile to consider some of the elements that enter into the development of ego.

Ego Organization and Development

In establishing a style of work, the individual manifests the state of his ego organization. Reflected in this organization are the impact on personality of the identifications with important figures in the individual's personal history. Successively, the mother, father, teachers, and later authority figures provide the building blocks out of which a unique ego may emerge.

Coupled with the identifications with models, the ego also contains the residues of competences and interests that the individual has cultivated, learned, and expressed in the course of his life history. These competences reflect his consitutional endowment and the way it enters into transactions with the environment. Did the individual activate talents, cultivate them and express them in ways that resulted in rewards from his environment? If so, these successive experiences of producing and being rewarded help form a core sense of self-esteem and a basic knowledge about the

[9] William James, *Varieties of Religious Experience* (New York: New American Library, Mentor Books, 1958).

talents one has and those one does not have. This sense of self-esteem yields a tendency to seek situations and experiences where one can make the greatest use of himself. I have preferred in other contexts to call this tendency "leading from strength" rather than weakness.

It is paradoxical, yet borne out by observation, that the tendency to lead from strength is a developmental gain that assures continued growth. The reverse, leading from weakness, reflects a developmental failure where a stage in the person's history resulted in unsolved problems of significant proportions. The learning process failed, and the individual in an effort to master the unsolved problems seeks in his current reality to repeat the experiences of the past, but usually with the same negative outcome.[10]

Another relevant aspect of ego organization is the nature of the individual's defenses and the balance of energy available for work and human relationships. Psychic energy, its biological derivations and the process by which it becomes converted into action, remains a mystery in psychology. Psychoanalytic theory assumes that a basic energy reservoir exists undifferentiated as an aspect of biological endowment.[11] In the course of development, energy becomes free of developmental conflicts and is available to the ego for goal-directed activity and expressivity.[12]

A certain portion of the available energy becomes engaged in defensive processes to control anxiety that arises from dangers of inner conflicts.[13] The ego defenses are a normal and necessary part of ego development, but when a disproportinate share of available energy is utilized in defending against anxiety, then presumably less is available for utilization in need satisfaction and work. Under these conditions, the individual functions with rela-

---

[10] S. Freud, *Beyond the Pleasure Principle* (London: International Psychoanalytical Press, 1922).

[11] S. Freud, *The Ego and the Id* (London: Hogarth Press, 1927).

[12] H. Hartmann, *Ego Psychology and the Problem of Adaptation* (New York: International Universities Press, 1958).

[13] S. Freud, *The Ego and Mechanisms of Defense* (London: Hogarth Press, 1937.)

tively severe constriction of the ego and is inhibited in work as well as human relationships.

The state of the ego as reflected in identification, expression of talents, and energy utilization is an outcome of development. Psychoanalytic theory views development as a function of a biologically determined timetable in which the activation of needs and their gratification proceed according to a pattern of shifting bodily functions. The bodily functions become the centers of the demands for gratification, the attachment to need-satisfying objects, and the demands of society for control of impulses.[14] Each stage in development helps to establish the conditions under which the successive life stages are experienced gradually linking life tasks to a complex organization of personality.

The three types of emotional investments of individuals (person-oriented, idea- or task-oriented, and fusion-oriented) represent the center of outward concern of the ego. These concerns are a product of the ego structure involving identification, expression of talents, and the utilization of energy. There is some evidence suggesting how ego structure and function are related to the orientations that distinguish one individual from another. It would be useful to cite some of this evidence, although it must be viewed as highly tentative at this stage.[15]

In terms of identifications, the person-oriented individual tends to have been far more influenced by the feminine figures in his life than by the masculine. His dominant identification trend is passive feminine. Just how this trend occurs is subject to alternate explanations ranging from excessive maternal dominance with relatively passive male influences in his development, to traumatic experiences in the infancy stages of development.

The identification patterns for the fusion types represent the results of parents who tended to minimize role differentiation. Both parents were capable of and showed affection and nurtur-

---

[14] S. Freud, *Three Essays on the Theory of Sexuality* (London: Imago, 1949). E. H. Erikson, "Identity and the Life Cycle," *Psychological Issues*, Vol. I, No. 1 (1959), pp. 18-49.

[15] Moment and Zaleznik, *op. cit.*, Zaleznik, Dalton and Barnes, *op. cit.*

ance while exercising influence and dominance. In the case of the idea set, parental role differentiation appeared sharply drawn along classical lines. The mother appeared affectionate and nurturant, while the father appeared distant, cold, but also influential in the course of development. The distant father should not be confused with the laissez-faire father. The idea set suggests a strong identification with a cold father who himself represented an earlier version of an idea type who invests himself in tasks rather than persons in his work orientation.

In terms of expression of talents, the idea type appears to have a strong sense of competence and self-worth, although it may manifest itself later in life than in the case of the fusion type. In our culture, the idea man achieves recognition relatively late simply because in the earlier stages of childhood and adolescence gregariousness seems to be rewarded. The idea man tends to show a history of individual work, while his counterpart in the fusion type excels in sports and group activity, but not necessarily to the exclusion of good school work. The talents of the fusion type involve being with others in cooperative activity.

The person-oriented individual's talents are not too clearly established. While appearing congenial in interpersonal settings and valued as a friend, he is less valued for leadership and work functions. It is important to note in this connection the fact that a male who is strongly person-oriented may not achieve or perform well largely because his activity may be incongruent with the types of performances that yield productivity and receive the more tangible rewards. Furthermore, a male whose dominant identifications are passive-feminine may suffer from considerable self-doubting and reduced self-esteem.

Self-esteem is built in large part through intimate experience with the cycle of productivity and reward as a result of the activation of talents. An individual acts and produces; he is evaluated and rewarded. This simple two-step cycle is important for building competence and self-esteem. We should not ignore the significance of environmental opportunities in this cycle because it is here that we see the effects of relative deprivations associated with membership in the lower social classes. Individuals with backgrounds in lower socioeconomic classes generally have less environmental opportunity and consequently less direct experience with a productivity-reward cycle that is free of anxiety.

With the introduction of the concept of anxiety, let us examine briefly the energy utilization processes in ego development as it relates to the three orientations under consideration. I suggested earlier that energy available for work, interpersonal or otherwise, is derived from the energy that is neutralized and freed of internal conflict. Available energy is also a function of the defensive requirements of the ego in its efforts to ward off anxiety and to deal with inner conflicts. No individual can be free of anxiety and a system of defenses. Nevertheless, an excessive proportion of energy diverted for defensive purposes results in inhibited functions and constricted activity.

There is a variety of evidence to suggest some of the patterns of defense characteristic of the person, fusion, and idea orientations. The person type defends against conflict and aggression. The conscious attitudes are generally altruistic as against egoistic with strong identification with the underdog. The idea type supports aggression but defends against intimacy and the more tender and ambiguous feelings frequently encountered in human interaction. The fusion type may have less rigidly constructed defenses than the other two types because of the tendency to rely on their closeness of fit with the environment to help in managing conflict. The fusion type, being strongly "socialized," accepts responsibility and related guilt feelings. Responsibility and the potential for guilt counter instinctual wishes and impulsive behavior. When the defenses related to accepting responsibility become excessive, one observes in fusion type individuals evidences of strong guilt and even depression.[16] This defensive aspect of responsibility is even more significant if it becomes tied to fear of loss of love and approval and rejection by the community.

This brief and somewhat oversimplified discussion of ego pro-

[16] Moment and Zaleznik, *op. cit.*, chap. 7.

cesses in the three orientations serves as a foundation for the later consideration of the development of interpersonal competence through educational procedures. Before I consider this issue more directly, there is one further step necessary to this discussion.

We have indicated so far the existence of at least three classes of executive functions that are tied to organization structures: homeostatic, mediative, and proactive. These functions define the shifting emphasis of managerial behavior from concern with internal processes (homeostatic) to concern with changing the environment (proactive). We have also examined (in relation to the individual who assumes a managerial role) the developmental issues that affect the condition of the ego as it presents itself in the work career. Here were differentiated three personality orientations that seem to determine the particular way an individual builds his career as an outgrowth of his history and experience. These personality orientations were called person, fusion, and idea, to describe patterns of emotional investments.

The important question this discussion raises is the interrelations between the executive functions in organizations and personality orientations of individuals. Can we foresee, even if only speculatively, how the various personality orientations might predispose individuals in the direction of one or more executive functions as intrinsic features of their style of work?

PERSONALITY ORIENTATIONS AND EXECUTIVE FUNCTIONS

One approach to these questions follows from arranging the two classes of variables in the form of a matrix, as presented in Figure 2 below.

The matrix in Figure 2 permits us to ask several questions: (1) Would there be a tendency for an individual with a dominant personality orientation to select for specialization one of the three executive functions? (2) What types of interpersonal performances are represented by the various specializations? (3) From the point of view of organizational effectiveness, does optimal managerial behavior imply the capacity for flexibility in interper-

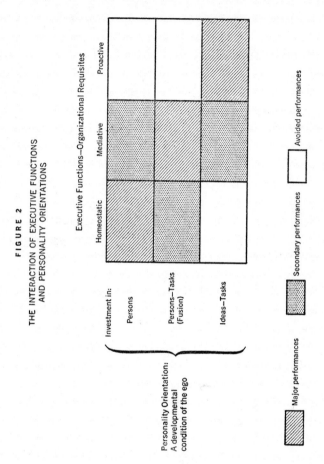

FIGURE 2

THE INTERACTION OF EXECUTIVE FUNCTIONS AND PERSONALITY ORIENTATIONS

sonal performances, or is it necessary for the functions to be performed within a constellation of executive roles patterned in the ways described in Chapter 8? (4) From the point of view of individual development through the career years, should emphasis be placed on flexibility in performances and consequently in modifications of the underlying personality orientations? or (5) Does individual development proceed more fruitfully by optimizing performance within an individual's existing personality?

One can only speculate on the answers to these questions since they actually indicate new avenues for investigation rather than issues that can be decided on the basis of existing evidence.

It would seem that the personality orientations lead to performance within specialized functions. This idea is expressed by the shadings within each cell in Figure 2. While every individual in his interpersonal relations has some degree of flexibility to adapt to various tasks and situations, each orientation would appear to be aimed selectively toward a particular function.

The person-oriented individual would perform most easily in the range of interpersonal behaviors associated with the homeostatic functions. I assume that such an individual would, relatively speaking, avoid proactive functions. Under conditions where proaction was thrust upon him and avoidance became difficult, the defensive apparatus of the individual would be under marked stress.

The idea-oriented individual, on the other hand, would perform most easily in the proactive functions, utilizing aggression and dominance as major components of his interpersonal style. Presumably, the homeostatic functions are not well understood by a proactive individual and may be strongly avoided.

To continue these speculations, organizational effectiveness would seem to require some mix in the performance of executive functions to assure both the securing of purpose and the maintenance of the internal capacities of the organization. Talcott Parsons and R. F. Bales, two Harvard social scientists, express this most clearly in their view of a social system.[17] The achievement of a purpose, or work, requires the release of energy, the engagement in aggressive-competitive activity directed toward solving problems. This activity results in a build-up of tension that, beyond a certain level, must be discharged to assure the continuity of the system. Tension release processes are closely related to the homeostatic functions discussed earlier. Activity in a social

[17] T. Parsons and R. F. Bales, *Family, Socialization and Interaction Process* (Glencoe, Free Press, 1955).

system, then, proceeds in cycles of tension build-up and tension release. This broad hypothesis suggests that the absence of relevant executive functions can result in the reduction of organizational effectiveness.

MODELS OF INTERPERSONAL COMPETENCE

There are, therefore, two main competing views available for exploring the structure and dynamics of executive performances. As a result of experimental work with small groups in problem-solving activity, Bales and his associates present the view that the effectiveness of a social system depends on a distribution of functions to appropriate specialists.[18] The task specialist exercises leadership through task performances: the social specialist exercises leadership through his efforts to restore the balance in the system by emotional expressivity and tension release. This view sees leadership as occurring in a bipartite distribution of executive functions as described in the preceding chapter.

The bipartite model is basic insofar as it also represents the structure of the nuclear family where the maternal figure is equivalent to the social specialist and the paternal figure to the task specialist. This model may well be oversimplified, yet it presents an excellent point of departure for the exploration and analysis of performances in organizations.[19]

The alternate view presents organizational effectiveness as the result of flexible performances by individuals who are capable of responding according to the demands of the situation.[20] Advocates of this view start with the assumption that functional re-

[18] R. F. Bales, "The Equilibrium Problem in Small Groups," *op. cit.*, pp. 111-161; P. E. Slater, "Role Differentiations in Small Groups;" A. P. Hare, E. F. Borgatta, and R. F. Bales, *Small Groups* (New York: Alfred A. Knopf, 1955), pp. 498-515.

[19] See R. C. Hodgson, D. J. Levinson, and A. Zaleznik, *The Executive Role Constellation: An Analysis of Personality and Role Relations in Management* (Boston: Division of Research, Harvard University Graduate School of Business Administration, 1965).

[20] K. D. Benne and P. Sheats, "Functional Roles of Group Members," *Journal of Social Issues*, Vol. IV, No. 2 (Spring, 1948), pp. 41-49.

quirements of an organization are of two kinds: task and maintenance. But, rather than establishing joint leadership according to the bipartite principle of specialization, they develop the view that both organizational effectiveness and individual development are enhanced under conditions of distributive leadership, where the organization permits all members to become flexible in their interpersonal performances and to meet the changing situational requirements.

This view is most closely associated with the group dynamics movement, but is also an accepted premise of most workers in the human relations field, whether or not they are students of Kurt Lewin and his followers.[21] These two positions lead to many significant comparisons including the values implicit in each, their scientific validity, implications for a theory of interpersonal behavior in organizations, and implications for management education and development.

MANAGEMENT EDUCATION AND DEVELOPMENT

Depending on which of the two views one adopts, the implications for management education and development differ. The theory of role specialization would not necessarily attempt to establish one ideal of role flexibility. It would view performances of the individual as an aspect of his ego function and character structure that are a product of lifelong development. The dynamics of development become the main sources for understanding the type of functions an individual assumes in his role as manager. To a certain extent most individuals do perform within a repertoire of performances with extreme specialization occurring under conditions of severe restrictions in personal develop-

[21] C. Argyris, *Interpersonal Competence and Organization Effectiveness* (Homewood, Ill.: Dorsey Press, and R. D. Irwin, 1962). L. P. Bradford, *et al., Explorations in Human Relations Training* (Washington, D. C.: National Training Laboratory in Group Development, 1953). F. J. Roethlisberger, *et al., Training for Human Relations* (Boston: Division of Research, Harvard Graduate School of Business Administration, 1954).

ment. To broaden further the range of behavior, however, may in and of itself require marked alterations in personality structure that are not feasible within the limits of educational processes, and that are not necessarily desirable. Role specialization then is viewed as a condition *within which* education seeks to improve interpersonal performance. To attempt to achieve competence otherwise ignores the paths of individual development and may involve ill-advised direct attempts at shifting the defensive and adaptive balance the individual has achieved in his personality.

A further position in role specialization views interpersonal performances in relation to the individual's stage in the life cycle. The young man embarking on a managerial career will most likely be sensitive to social processes because of his own needs for security and membership. A shift can occur in his performances beginning with the early thirties where he stresses, relatively speaking, ideas and technical functions, rather than social process. Other shifts can also occur during other periods in his career development.

Attempts at altering performance are contained within the individual's dominant personality orientation, reflecting also individual concerns and situational pressures that are specific to particular phases of development. One would, therefore, conclude that a single overriding objective of increased flexibility in functions performed would be difficult to achieve, if not irrelevant for certain stages in the career years of the life cycle.

The second view, that of role flexibility as a principle in education for interpersonal competence, assumes in the first place that situational forces are strategic in determining the manager's performance. The kind of organization in which one performs will establish through the structure of group standards permissive limits on behavior. By altering the standards, one achieves increased flexibility, especially through support from training methods and experiences.

Educational procedures following this second set of assumptions seek to establish an ideal type of organization based upon broad philosophical foundations of democracy and the scientific method.[22] With this ideal culture individual growth, which includes flexible performances and distributive leadership, flourishes.

The proponents of this second view, while placing the strategic factors for interpersonal competence within the organization, tend to ignore the developmental foundations of individual behavior. Their view is in keeping with a liberal tradition of social reform, but the object of the reform is the organization rather than the individual. How organizations or societies can change apart from individual change is still, however, an open question.

One further distinction between these individualistic-organizational frames of reference is important to consider, although it has been implied in earlier discussion. An individualistic frame of reference seeks to avoid the highly charged and abstract philosophical ideals characteristic of the organizational reform groups. Broad philosophical premises seem to become molds to which individuals have to adapt and in this sense are inconsistent with a philosophy of education for individual growth.

CONCLUSION

Professional education for a managerial career is rightfully concerned with issues of competence in the management of human affairs. It is here that the behavioral sciences may make a lasting contribution to business. A danger exists, however, when certain premises are accepted without critical scrutiny. One such set of premises seeks to establish criteria of interpersonal competence within a tradition of organizational and cultural reform, ignoring the significance of what has been learned of human development.

It is fallacious to describe the managerial role and interpersonal

[22] W. G. Bennis, "Towards a 'Truly' Scientific Management: The Concept of Organization Health," *Industrial Management Review*, Vol. IV, No. 1 (Fall, 1962), pp. 1-27.

behavior underlying it in terms of one set of ideals, especially a set of ideals that are attributes of a culture. There are many different types of managerial role performances that present different configurations of interpersonal behaviors. The validity of a performance can be understood in terms of its relation to ego development, not in its degree of conformity to cultural ideals. One set of behaviors that conforms to cultural ideals may exist at the expense of a tenuous internal balance in ego functioning. Another set of behaviors may violate certain tenets of good human relations practice, but represents a developmental continuity that builds successively upon new ego strengths. This latter position probably contains the greatest degree of validity and, in the final analysis, may result in a highly moral individual.

10 / *Management and the Behavioral Sciences*

Managers are increasingly faced with the problem of evaluating the effects of the behavioral sciences on business organizations and management practice. Sometimes this need for evaluation arises because of a specific proposal to undertake a management development or consultation program, or to introduce new methods of work based on behavioral science applications. At times the interest is provoked by management's search for solutions to pressing problems. In any case, managers have long been aware of the possible mutual impact of behavioral sciences and management through research, publication of articles and the development of curricula in business schools.

The purpose of this chapter is to: (1) provide a historical perspective on why the behavioral sciences are at the forefront, along with mathematics, in new directions in management; (2) present the critical issues in applications; (3) present alternate views on the most fruitful lines of future application.

The main ideas of this chapter emphasize the important differences between the job of the manager and the behavioral scientist. As a result of these differences there is no direct application of behavioral science knowledge apart from the capacity of the manager to make judgments and to choose actions. Both the manager *and* the behavioral scientist need to avoid utopianism and the confusion between social research and social action. The behavioral sciences have an effect on organizations mainly through education and consultation as these influence individual judgment and action. There is no ideal form of organization or management behavior to be fostered by the behavioral sciences, but only sets of alternatives each with its own payouts and costs. The behavioral sciences will illuminate these alternatives and their respective values and costs, but the manager will still be the agent of choice and commitment.

HISTORICAL PERSPECTIVES

The decade of the 1950s marked the start of a new development for management as a profession. This development fostered the concept of management as an applied social science. Individuals preparing themselves for a career in management and those already experienced in this professional role became increasingly aware of the limitations of common sense in the achievement of competence as a practitioner. They joined the company of men who throughout history have had the courage to examine practice somewhat self-consciously, to see its strengths and shortcomings, and to turn to new modes of exploration in the pursuit of competence in their career.

The universities, and more specifically the graduate schools of business, were the centers of the development of applied social science in relation to management. The motive power and support for this work came from the foundations culminating in the publication of two studies on the state of curriculum development in business schools. One report, authored by Gordon and Howell,[1] resulted from a study sponsored by the Ford Foundation. The second, authored by Pierson,[2] appeared under the auspices of the Carnegie Foundation. These two reports and a

[1] Robert A. Gordon and James E. Howell, *Higher Education to Business* (New York: Columbia University Press, 1959).
[2] Pierson, Frank C., *et al.*, *The Education of Seminar Businessmen* (New York: McGraw-Hill Book Company, 1959).

more recent study sponsored by the Committee for Economic Development led to much discussion and self-examination within the university.[3] The reports agreed that one foundation of education for management in the future lay in the application of the behavioral sciences and mathematics to the problems of decision making in organized human settings.

While the business education reports in no way matched the dramatic impact on management that the Flexner report of the early 1900s had on medicine, one could not help but draw certain parallels between the two. At the turn of the century, education for medicine labored under extremely poor standards, with considerable reliance on the authority of precedent and existing practice as the sole guidelines for content and expertise in an important profession. The Flexner report, produced under the formal auspices of the Rockefeller Foundation, became a model for those efforts that attempt to change society through improvements in education. What may not be so widely understood, however, is how much the Flexner report depended for its success upon the prior establishment of medicine at the core of the biological and experimental sciences. Claude Bernard, the nineteenth-century experimentalist, became known as the father of modern medicine largely through his persistent elaboration of the scientific methods in the study of physiology and disease.[4] In an even more fundamental sense, Flexner's report depended upon the evolution of science as the stamp of Western civilization, a point of view discussed by the eminent philosopher Alfred North Whitehead in his book, *Science and the Modern World*.[5]

Flexner's report became historic because the ground had been made fertile for his ideas in large part through the work of men of science. Following his report, schools of medicine became the institutional centers for the proliferation of this point of view

[3] Report of the Committee on Economic Development, "Educating Tomorrow's Managers" (New York, 1964).

[4] Claude Bernard, *An Introduction to the Study of Experimental Medicine* (New York: Dover Publications, 1957).

[5] Alfred North Whitehead, *Science and the Modern World* (London: Williams & Norgate, 1955).

and led to major revisions in medical education and in the dedication to research as a way of developing a humanitarian profession.

I cite the parallel between the 1950s in management education and the 1900s in medicine for purposes of drawing some crucial comparisons. To make the parallels complete, let us ask ourselves several questions: What promise does the future hold for the enrichment of management as a profession in the application of the behavioral sciences? In what sense and in what ways can the research efforts of the specialists in the human sciences alter the practice of managers charged with the responsibility of achieving high levels of effectiveness of men at work in organizations? This question requires searching examination of the trends in the ideologies and theories of management as these create the underpinnings of organizational practice.[6]

Ideologies and Theories of Management

Concurrent with the renewed discussions of the 1950s described before, we find a series of negative developments. The existing theories and ideologies of management had largely run their course of usefulness as the foundations of a profession. The scientific management movement under the leadership of Frederick Taylor provided for the first quarter or more of the twentieth century a basic theory. Viewing work in organizations as a function of energy utilization, Taylor and others applied the technique of observation and measurement to secure a more rational way of allocating the application of human energy in conjunction with the use of tools. This theory found application in the specializations of industrial engineering and personnel management, but also as an underlying conceptual approach to line management. The great gap in this theoretical system lay in its inability to explain certain pervasive facts about human behavior. It is true that scientific management provided for a structure of

[6] See James G. March and Herbert A. Simon, *Organizations* (New York: John Wiley and Sons, 1958).

rewards for work based upon certain concepts of motivation and learning. Yet these concepts were not subjected to the same empirical test used in the studies of energy utilization. It was not until the famous Hawthorne studies that serious consideration was given to the nature of motivation at work and the system of human relationships within which motives find expression.

The intent of the investigations in scientific management and the Hawthorne studies was to provide an improved framework for the management of work, particularly at the blue-collar and the lower levels of the white-collar occupations in organizations. As for the ideas concerning the structure of work at the reaches of power in organizations, a theory parallel to scientific management existed in the concepts of the rationalists like Fayol, and in the tradition of military thinkers and bureaucratic theorists. This theory is exemplified best in the concepts of specialization of function and the span of control. These concepts provided a basis for rational planning of organization structure: to optimize the efforts of managers and to secure the most efficient system of coordination and communication. In practice, such organization theory found its way into the development of organization charts, the job description, and other like instruments of personnel management.

Following upon the Hawthorne studies and other investigations of human behavior in organizations, serious questions came to the fore about the adequacy of rational bureaucratic concepts of organization. These concepts viewed the organization as the mold to which the individual shapes himself or adapts under the impetus of work incentives. But at the concrete level of empirical findings, investigators were calling attention to variations in behavior that suggested the existence of an informal organization. Observational studies of men at work showed that individuals varied considerably in the actual compared with the expected behavior. Instead of seeing the actual behavior as deviant forms, sociological investigators indicated that the informal organization served as a corrective device in permitting a wider range of need satisfaction than is possible with existing organizational requirements or rewards. The informal organization made it possible for bureaucratic systems to function even more effectively than in the absence of these so-called deviant practices. The famous Bank Wiring Room[7] study stands out as a pioneer in this regard, along with Peter Blau's exceptional field study of two government agencies reported in his book, *The Dynamics of Bureaucracy*.[8]

These social-psychological studies of organization brought into serious doubt the adequacy of rationalistic theories of organization. Again, they revealed limitations in the explanation of social-emotional phenomena readily observable in studies of behavior. Even the most casual observer of organizational behavior had to restate his questions to permit understanding of the complex forms of behavior and emotional experience of individuals at work. The answers to these questions could not be found in the reflections of the organizational rationalists.

Psychodynamic Theory

At this juncture, let us turn to another development in the human sciences of the first quarter of the twentieth century, one whose effects have not been fully realized yet in organization theory and practice. Laboring in Vienna at the turn of the century, a scientist trained initially in medicine displayed the most remarkable gifts of creativity in pursuing new ideas about how and why men behave in the way they do. Sigmund Freud made basic discoveries about human development and dynamics and presented these as the new psychoanalytic psychology.[9] This psychology is truly an individual psychology in that it selects for study the intrapsychic experience of the person. It establishes the existence and interrelation of three levels of experience and awareness—the conscious, the preconscious, and the unconscious

[7] F. J. Roethlisberger and W. J. Dickson, *Management and the Worker* (Cambridge: Harvard University Press, 1939).

[8] Peter M. Blau, *The Dynamics of Bureaucracy* (Chicago: University of Chicago Press, 1955).

[9] Ernest Jones, *The Life and Work of Sigmund Freud* (New York: Basic Books, 1953-1956).

—and opens the way for challenging explanations of motivation and behavior.

Freud worked within the unique laboratory of the psychoanalytic setting. His discoveries grew out of persistent observation and exploration within this setting. Yet his findings and theories provided significant leads for the study of many applied problems. His monograph, *Group Psychology and the Analysis of the Ego*,[10] for example, contains basic ideas on the phenomena of leadership and morale. His study of authority in *Totem and Taboo*[11] opens for investigation ideas about the structure of authority within organizations in relation to individual development, the control of impulses, and emotions.

In general, the application of psychoanalytic psychology to the study of organizations provides the lead for understanding unsolved problems left largely unattended in the rationalistic theories of organization. The essential point of departure in the psychoanalytic study of organizations can best be illustrated by posing the question of man's relation to organization and society. The primitive instinctual side of life must be educated and controlled to assure basic gratification of needs through work on the environment and human relationships. Mankind constantly faces the threat posed through the potential eruption of uncontrolled aggressive impulses in both individual and collective forms. The real lesson for society in the analysis of the war-torn period of the twentieth century with its unprecedented slaughter of innocent people has not yet been formulated and told. It remains to be told as an instance of the eruption of primitive forces that are at once attributable to the individual, yet capable of stimulation and discharge through collective behavior. A similar problem appears before us in the ever present threat of the bomb and its capacity for ending civilization as we know it.

The threat of primitive aggression and the efforts to control

[10] Sigmund Freud, *Group Psychology and the Analysis of the Ego*, Standard Edition (London: The Hogarth Press, 1955).
[11] Sigmund Freud, *Totem and Taboo*, Standard Edition (London: The Hogarth Press, 1955).

these forces exist as significant determinants of human organization. While certain forms of organization may serve to contain aggression and its derivatives, this control is not achieved without the payment of a large price in the human potential for creativity. Those who basically fear the underlying sources of human energy spend untold hours of their conscious awareness in elaborating ways to dampen aggression and its derivatives. There exist individuals who unwittingly stamp out creativity or the aspiration toward creativity largely through their own inability to deal flexibly with the issue of rivalry, whether in relation to peers or to authority figures. These individuals become the driving forces toward bureaucratization of man's relation to man to the point where organizational forms no longer serve a useful human purpose.

Creativity results in part from the fusion of human instincts, where the control and utilization of energy is taken over by the individual as his responsibility and not given over to external control. The dominant instinct in creative endeavor is love, the desire to make and create in the most elementary human sense. The forces of love dominate aggression and through transformation utilize these energies in creating. Mankind is thereby served in new ways and with a degree of grace unforetold in the conventional ideas of work.

Creativity in this sense may be found in many walks of life and in many endeavors. Here the individual remakes and enhances society rather than merely adapting to the constraints imposed upon him. One of the central issues facing organizational research and practice is to sort out the conclusions derived from study of the creative process and to apply these to the building and management of large-scale organizations.

The question of human creativity within large-scale organizations is central to the development of organization theory and practice in the future. Under present conditions individuals are creative despite rather than because of systems of organization. I am fully convinced that present-day organizations weigh heavily in the direction of control and have little positive impact on the creative process. Find an innovative organization in business or government and you will largely find the impact of the individual, who for complex reasons is able to transcend the conventional definitions of problems and role and who exerts an overwhelming effect on the thinking of others. In this connection, the study of the "great man" in history is exceedingly instructive.

One such study published by Erik H. Erikson as a contribution in psychoanalysis, and history presents an interpretation of the crucial transformation of Martin Luther. The essential theme in Erikson's *Young Man Luther*[12] is the effect of one individual's resolution of his identity crisis on the shape and course of history. Luther, torn between his destructive and passive wishes toward the father-figure and its representation in God and the church could not find the solution for himself in the conventional notions of obedience either to his real father or to the symbolic father. The revolt against his real father led him to the church, and a second revolt against the symbolic father provided him with a means to foster a new ideology and to alter the patterns of history. The route to this transformation lay in the final and complete acceptance of his own inner torment reflected finally in the ideological notion of faith. To profane the idea somewhat, faith meant that the grace of God could be known to the individual directly and would be expressed by his works on earth. Little prospect for salvation could be found through deeds or through the intercession of an established church. The individual could therefore hope to know God and His word directly without the intervention of a hierarchy. This ideology could only have emerged from an individual's struggle for knowledge of himself.

There are parallels to be drawn in the study of modern organization and leadership. Insofar as individuals use organizations mainly to control instinctual processes and their derivatives, we see the persistence of relatively conventional work. But where through education and insight the individual asserts self-control

[12] E. H. Erikson, *Young Man Luther* (New York: W. W. Norton 1958).

and assumes responsibility for his own inner processes then we see in nascency the work of transformation.

In reviewing the evolution of organization theory I have suggested that the unsolved problem in understanding man in organization centers around the inability of existing theory to grasp the essential dynamics of the individual and from this understanding to formulate a truly psychosocial theory of organization and leadership. Psychoanalytic psychology as a psychology of the individual has provided and continues to provide the lead in this direction; whether the lead is pursued remains to be seen. If my reading of current trends in organizational research is accurate, I would expect a significant movement ahead in the years to come. Such a development, however, will lead to many further problems in the application of knowledge to the work of the manager. Foremost among these problems is the effort to differentiate and relate the contrasting modes of exploration and action.

EXPLORATION AND ACTION

There is little question that the main impetus for the idea of management as applied social science has stemmed from the desire to improve the work of managers in business and government. This avid desire to improve the work of the practitioner is simultaneously a great source of strength and weakness in the application of behavioral research. The strengths come from the opportunities afforded researchers with applied interests in using organizations as laboratories and in finding the funds to support their work. The weakness exists in the behavioral scientist's tendency to become personally overextended in the zealous desire to make his knowledge work.

Among social researchers interested in organizational behavior there has been a marked tendency to discredit the tradition of pure research—the investigation of problems for their own intrinsic value and for the beauty of bringing order out of chaos through the formulation of ideas. I believe we discredit this tradition at our own peril. Research investigations that are not impelled by the zest for immediate application have profound impact upon the thinking of practitioners as well as on other investigators. The impact, however, takes time, but returnable time because of the enduring nature of the contributions.

But perhaps of more concern to us here than the conflict between pure and applied research in appraising the effects of social research on management is the distinction between the two types of theory impelling investigation: explanatory and normative theory. This distinction is so fundamental to our discussion that I would like to explore it in some detail.

Explanatory and Normative Theory

Explanatory theory consists of propositions about behavior that incorporate most economically the wide range of facts under study. Normative theory consists of statements that indicate how an individual *should* behave to realize certain desired ends. An illustration of an explanatory proposition is the following:

Satisfaction varies directly with environmental returns and inversely with individual needs. This proposition attempts to explain why individuals vary in their degree of felt satisfaction with organizational rewards. Two individuals with the same degree of social acceptance in a group, for example, may express widely differing responses because one individual has a strong need for social acceptance while the other has weak desires in this respect. Or, as another illustration, two individuals with equal opportunities for autonomy may respond quite differently depending on their need for autonomy.

This explanatory proposition regarding satisfaction and morale has been found to hold true in the widest range of circumstances and cases. For example, in studies of responses of individuals to promotion rates in the military during the Second World War men in the military police were found to be quite satisfied with promotion while those in the air corps expressed relative dissatisfaction despite the fact that promotion rates in the air corps exceeded those in the military police. The difference is understood in the greater desire and expectation of promotion for air corps men compared with the military police.[13]

As another illustration from a study of executive motivation and satisfaction, we found that executives with a high need for achievement responded with the lowest expressed satisfaction with all aspects of their job and career as compared with executives whose needs for achievement were relatively low. The differences result from the states of motivation rather than in varying degrees of environmental reward.[14]

In still another study of motivation and satisfaction, in this case of factory workers, we found that individuals who expressed the greatest degree of satisfaction with their group membership were those who were actually accepted members of the dominant group and who positively identified with the group. The identification served as a motivation to belong that was satisfied through actual membership. Among the less satisfied individuals were those who were accepted by the group but who sought membership in higher status groups outside the factory and among the middle-class population.[15]

While some social scientists and managers may express interest in the explanatory propositions such as the one just illustrated, they may also voice two kinds of discontent: the first, expressed typically by the social scientist who seeks to change the world, is that the proposition does not explain enough; the second type of discontent asks the action question more directly in the form of "So what?" Suppose this proposition were accepted, then what would anyone do who had an interest in increasing morale, or gaining higher productivity levels through the manipulation of job satisfactions.

[13] S. A. Stouffer, et. al., The American Soldier, Vol. 1: Adjustment During Army Life (Princeton: Princeton University Press, 1949).

[14] A. Zaleznik, and D. Moment, The Dynamics of Interpersonal Behavior (New York: John Wiley and Sons, 1964).

[15] A. Zaleznik, C. R. Christensen, and F. J. Roethlisberger, The Motivation, Productivity and Satisfaction of Workers: A Prediction Study (Cambridge: Division of Research, Harvard Graduate School of Business Administration, 1958).

The response to the first type of discontent is that no proposition will explain everything. The scientist who is able to formulate a proposition from which he may then derive a whole set of new and exciting questions should count himself lucky. The second discontent has only one answer: one cannot derive a normative statement from an explanatory proposition through logic. To put it another way, how a manager should behave given existing knowledge about human behavior in organizations does not derive directly from the body of concepts and findings that make up this knowledge. Action implies choice and the weighing of consequences, a process that lends itself to scientific study, but not to externally derived imperatives unless one happens to be interested in theology.

To pursue this point further, we must turn to the nature of normative theory, how it is established in the first place, the means by which it is communicated, its utilities and weaknesses, and its relation to explanatory theory.

The Nature of Normative Theory

The simplest and most widely cited normative proposition in management practice is the principle of span of control, and this somewhat overworked and badly maligned principle will serve us well as an illustration.[16] The principle says that a manager should supervise no more than seven subordinates. The key word in the normative proposition is *should*, the imperative that certain desirable consequences will follow and other undesirable ones be avoided if an individual conforms in his behavior to the principle. The way the normative principle of span of control, along with similar principles, becomes established is through the experience and wisdom of practitioners who hand these ideas down until they become articulated and given a name. The normative principle is quite different from the explanatory proposition in that it does not become established through formal observation and test.

[16] Herbert Simon, *Administrative Behavior* (New York: The Macmillan Company, 1958), chap. 2.

It stands as part of the collective wisdom of a profession. How normative propositions develop, of course, is no indication of their utility or truth. They may be quite useful guides to behavior or misleading under certain circumstances. The important point for our purposes is that if managers act on the normative principles as though they were scientific propositions, they are inviting trouble.

The normative proposition asserts how an individual should behave to realize certain ends; an explanatory proposition describes and accounts for the relations among phenomena, or how people actually behave. There is no direct traffic between normative and explanatory theory. To convert a normative into an explanatory statement, one would have to test and describe the conditions under which the action proposed leads or does not lead to the consequences anticipated. This step involves the application of observational-experimental methods and a frame of reference quite different from that which is characteristic of men who enjoy dealing in normative theories.

The reverse traffic, deriving a normative from an explanatory proposition, as indicated previously, involves individual choice, the expression of values, the attachment to goals, the willingness to endure certain costs to realize other ends—all qualities of an educated and mature mind.

The future of behavioral science applications to management depends on the development of a coherent relationship between normative and explanatory frames of thought, between the world of scientific behavior and managerial behavior. The future, if any, of the dialogue between these two worlds will depend on asserting and maintaining this coherent relationship. The relationship I envision is one of role specialization and separation. The jobs of the manager and the behavioral scientist studying management and organizations are different.

The job of the behavioral scientist, on the one hand, is to develop the explanations of behavior and to communicate these to interested persons in the community. I assume the manager is among those vitally interested persons. The job of the manager, on the other hand, is to behave *as though* he had a body of normative theory to govern his actions. In other words, the manager acts out of conviction born from thinking, experimenting, testing and, above all, choosing.

The Roles of the Manager and the Behavioral Scientist

I believe, if it were possible to attain this ideal of role separation and complementation, we would witness considerable progress in both the study of organizational behavior and the practice of management. The behavioral scientist would be able to extricate himself from the several impossible positions into which he may have wandered. One such position is that of the utopian, who from a limited base of ideas formulates a social movement designed to change the culture of formal organizations.

Social change in society has very special historic and contemporary meaning. Some of the finest aspirations of our national experience have been realized through the ability of leaders to give voice to inequity and injustice wherever it is found. But social change and social science are not the same. I view with considerable pessimism the attempts, for example, to develop a social movement around thoeries of permissive leadership, participation, and sensitivity training.

Researches on participation and permissive leadership have in fact shown in certain instances beneficial effects on morale and productivity. But just as psychiatry, one intellectual parent of most theories of permissive leadership, had to discover painfully the illusory quality of the transference cure, so are organization theorists discovering the ephemeral nature of these positive findings. The research setting creates the condition for the redistribution of emotional investments that affect the levels of productivity and morale. When the researchers leave the setting or the original effects wear off, another redistribution takes effect that may result in, at best, a return to the prior situation or at worst cynical and disillusioned individuals.

The emergence of sensitivity training (the T-Group)[17] as an idealized form of organization and interaction is also questionable in my view. The attempt here is to alter the power relations in organizations through the introduction of new norms of behavior incorporated within the egalitarian ideology of the peer group. Man has known since time immemorial of the dilemmas of power. The solution of power crises by its shift from individuals to a group contains its own seeds of decay. The positive side of power is in its coexistence with a sense of responsibility in individuals. Groups do not take responsibility, only men. The absorption of power without responsibility leads to stalemate and failure in work.

Another view of sensitivity training offers this procedure as a means for changing individuals. This view also falls short of the reality in back of the question of how and why individuals change. The motivational conditions under which persons enter into training groups and the time involved in the typical experience both limit severely the degree of individual change possible.

Turning to the outcomes for managers of confusion between science and action, there exists a tendency for managers to look mainly outside of themselves for guides in governing their behavior. This tendency can exist in any profession and is not restricted to management. As soon as any manager uses the results of research as the basic justification for his behavior he faces important difficulties. He cannot act with confidence and the sense of direction that comes from knowing that one is utilizing to the utmost his personal capacities and sense of competence. This competence is not built from without as though skills can be grafted onto the individual to make him into something that he cannot become.

No set of normative principles substitutes in any action profession for the individual's sense of wholeness in exercising talents and dispositions that he knows for sure are his own. The norma-

[17] Sensitivity and the T-Group are names given to various forms of training in group dynamics.

tive principles can assert socially valued ideals, whether couched in the convictions of democracy or of science. If they exist for the individual apart from himself and as imperatives to which he must conform slavishly, then we will find a guilt-ridden and compulsive personality.

The explanatory theories of science cannot be transformed directly into normative principles of action. The behavioral scientist should at the outset be clear about this in his own mind and not unwittingly foster an illusion. The practicing manager should also avoid treating normative propositions as though these spoke with the authority of science.

The attempt to distinguish between explanatory and normative theory and to urge the avoidance of confusion of roles between the scientist and the manager does not in any way imply pessimism on this writer's part about the future possibilities growing out of the dialogue between the behavioral scientist and the manager. At the outset of this chapter it was indicated that the shift in focus of the schools of business and the introduction of behavioral sciences through research and teaching contain important meanings for the future. Let us now turn to the applications ahead and the ways in which the manager and the behavioral scientist can each contribute further to the evolution of a profession.

FUTURE APPLICATIONS

The direction of the applications of behavioral science to management is twofold: (1) through education; (2) through consultation.

Education

Education for management is part of the tradition of professional education which, over all, has not had an extensive history. The traditional means of professional education has been the apprenticeship, the practice of the arts of the profession under the guidance of the experienced master. With the results of knowledge accumulated through research and the codification of practice, formal education in the profession attempts to reduce but not to eliminate the apprenticeship period and to improve the quality of later on-the-job experience through the foundation provided by the formal education. The extent to which the educational procedures use the results of scientific investigation result in a unique educational experience.

Education has had and continues to have one overriding objective. Its aims are to enrich the individual, to make him strong and free through the development of competences. The behavioral sciences can fruitfully work within this philosophy of education applied to the profession of management. By concentrating on the communication of knowledge and the enhancing of competence, the behavioral sciences are able to resolve the dilemma I referred to earlier between the generation of knowledge in the form of explanatory propositions and the action of individuals based on normative propositions. The resolution of this dilemma lies in fostering the position of inquiry as a normative ideal. In a practical sense social science knowledge can provide the manager with a range of diagnostic and analytic ideas and with a set of indicators that can enhance his perception and depth of understanding of organizational issues.

A good example of how valuable ideas grow out of social research is provided in the study, *The Dynamics of Bureaucracy*, by Peter Blau, briefly referred to earlier in this chapter. Blau's study, in part, examined the relationship between productivity and statistical performance reports of the type used commonly in measuring and appraising output. The study took place in a state employment agency, and productivity consisted of successful job placements, serving both applicants for jobs and employers with vacancies.

The basic concept of general value used in this study is the *unanticipated consequences of action*. Managers act to secure certain intended objectives. In the employment agency the intended effect of the statistical reports was to increase the interviewer's motivation to produce by activating competitive attitudes through the comparisons made visible in the reports. In other words, the management used a common working hypothesis that higher productivity would result from intensification of competitiveness as an inducement to produce.

The *unanticipated consequence* of introducing the statistical records was to lower productivity in one section where competitiveness increased while productivity increased in a second section where competitiveness *did not* increase. The basic differences in response of the two sections related to how the supervisors used the records. In the case of the lowered productivity, the supervisor in fact acted to increase competitiveness. This resulted in a positive correlation between individual competitiveness and productivity—the more the individual competed, the more he produced. But this correlation between competitiveness and productivity existed at the expense of lowered group productivity. One individual's increased productivity was countered by someone else's reduced productivity.

This effect did not occur in the second section because the supervisor modified the use of the statistical reports to encourage improvement in the productivity record of the group as a whole.

The concept of unanticipated consequences leads to intensive diagnosis and analysis of objectives, procedures, and motivational effects. Such analysis presumably should lead to clearer decisions and the warding off of undesirable side effects.

This example represents the type of psychosocial inquiry that can enter into the education of managers. You will note that the explanations in this analysis do not directly provide normative prescriptions. The manager cannot directly or easily infer what individual action should be taken in relation to the problem of productivity and competitiveness in organizations.

The behavioral scientist may, and hopefully will, go on to study and experiment with the effects of different kinds of management on productivity. But here again, these experiments provide new knowledge, leaving the question of action as part of the process of decision and responsibility on the part of the individual manager. The analysis and the knowledge deepens the perceptivity of the individual, provides for him paths of experimental behavior, but does not offer direct prescriptions.

The essence of action is in choice. Choosing as an inherent ego function is susceptible to wide variations in behavior and commitments that reflect the differences in style of individuals, and also the types of organizational problems encountered. In my view, there is no single favored remedy to organizational problems. The range of alternatives is wide, each implying a different set of rewards and costs that must be weighed and balanced by individuals. It is this view of choice that ultimately sets the individual free and that permits him to use knowledge in the sense of inquiry. The stress is on the individual and his learning and development. To repeat an earlier observation, education is for the individual and never for the institution or organization. We hope that organizations gain, but only through the enhancement experienced in relation to the competences exercised by educated and free men.

The social scientist who takes the utopian position and seeks an ideal form of organizational culture within which people function, a view contrary to that of individual education, will find that he exerts only a new type of stress on individuals who still must act within the framework of their own developmental problems. We may find emerging a popular trend in management and organizations, but these innovations in the form of social movements run their course and become further historical testimony to the idea that the *basic issue in life is the individual and the use he makes of himself in his struggle for a sense of wholeness.*

Consultation

The second direction for application of behavioral science knowledge is in consultation. Consultation occurs when one individual gives help to another by exercising a specialized competence. This competence unfolds in a relationship to another individual who experiences problems in the activation of his competence, and in the discharge of his responsibilities. The consultant role for the behavioral scientist as here defined has yet to be realized fully because of a variety of difficulties introduced by both consultants and clients.

The basic competence the behavioral scientist has to offer the manager is the range of knowledge he commands, the expertise in the use of methods of investigation, and specialized clinical ability in offering help through the process of inquiry. You may question whether many behavioral scientists have these talents available for taking on the responsibility of consultation. Whether many exist or not, the requirements still exist for the types of abilities just outlined.

The reason consultation works well in those cases we can cite as positive examples is because both the consultant and the client are prepared to enter into an appropriate psychosocial contract. I have had clients or potential clients come to me, for example, with the invitation to undertake work with them under conditions where the client in effect offers to help the consultant. A favorite indicator of this misapprehension of what consultation is about occurs when the client says something like this: "We have some very interesting situations that I think you can learn a lot from. Why don't you come in and have a look." My response typically is, "Why are *you* here? What are *your* problems? How do you think I can help *you?*"

The appropriate consultation relationship exists where the client defines himself, with every ounce of emotional energy at his command, in need of help as a responsible person in an organization. The consultant may be a person who needs help too, but if he does it is his responsibility to get the help from an appropriate individual and not to use ostensible consultation relationships to solve his problems. Nor should he allow himself to be seduced into a vague situation with the words, "Come in and have a look at some interesting problems."

Another aspect of the relationship inappropriate to consultation is the initiation of the contract by the consultant in selling a package that is supposed to be good for all organizations. Here the consultant may even sell his services in the form of research and pay part or all of the costs out of his own funds. Under these conditions I think we get neither good research nor effective consultation. The initial presence of an individual who defines himself as in need of help is elementary and the *sine qua non* for any type of consultation, including the use of the behavioral scientist.

I believe that much fruitful application of social science knowledge is possible through effective consultation. There can emerge some very useful work on the problems of the organization and incidental to this work, we usually find that individuals learn a great deal.

The success or failure of consultation contracts frequently turn on the particular types of power issues that enmesh individuals in organizations. Groups within the organization may attempt to use the consultant to foster their cause in a power struggle with some other group. The basic objectivity of the consultant, one of his potentially valuable contributions to the process, may be seriously impaired if he takes up the cudgels and defines his client within a provincial struggle for assertion and control. This possibility comes closer to actuality as the behavioral sciences become invested as status symbols.

Conclusion

The main purpose of this chapter has been to present a perspective on the relationship of the behavioral sciences to the management of large organizations. The impetus for this development has come from the university, largely as an outcome of the contest of ideas on the making of a profession. The issue here is the balance between accumulated experience and scientific knowledge in education for management. The contest in ideas occurred, as it does in all professions, when consensus emerges that existing philosophies and theories have run their course and have collided with brute realities that can no longer be overlooked. The existing philosophies at issue have been derived from three main sources: first, the scientific management movement; second, the rationalist theories of formal organizaton; third, the eclectic and pragmatic approaches to management. The way in which the behavioral sciences stand to make their greatest contribution is in the development of knowledge about the motivational, expressive, and developmental experience of man in organization. This view has application to the problem of action and decision in organization, the structure of formal organization, the introduction of change in organizations, career development, and the process of leadership.

Whatever knowledge we achieve will need to enter the dialogue between the scientist and the manager. This dialogue will proceed more vigorously if both sides to the interchange keep in mind the distinction between explanatory and normative propositions. Once this distinction is clouded in thinking, then the problems of the scientist and the practitioner become infinitely more complex. The scientist cannot tell the practitioner what to do; this question falls within the realm of individual choice and commitment. The practitioner cannot justify his action in the name of science or truth; he cannot evade his responsibility by cloaking himself with the mantle of objective truth. But the behavioral sciences and the spirit of inquiry at the heart of investigation can help the act of choice through the time-honored work of individual education and through consultation.

Finally, in the next chapter, it is appropriate to examine the problems and possibilities of education for individuality and the sense of responsibility.

11 / *The Myth of the Death of the Hero*

The Harvard Business Review carried an article entitled "Democracy Is Inevitable."[1] The authors of this piece, Warren Bennis and Philip Slater, are two social scientists who presented an interesting thesis that is especially useful as a point of departure for this concluding chapter.

Bennis and Slater believe that democratic organizations (especially business) are inevitable products of an evolutionary process that involves changing relationships between the individual and the organization. To quote the authors:

We are now beginning an era when a man's knowledge and approach can become obsolete before he has even begun the career for which he was trained. The value of what one learns is always slipping away, like the value of money in a runaway inflation of knowledge and skill, and it is this which is perhaps responsible for the feelings of futility, alienation, and lack of individual worth which are said to characterize our times.

Under such conditions, the individual *is* [authors' italics] of relatively little significance. No matter how imaginative, energetic, and brilliant he may be, time will soon catch up with him to the point where he can profitably be replaced by someone equally imaginative, energetic, and brilliant, but with a more up-to-date viewpoint and

[1] *Harvard Business Review*, Vol. 42, March-April, 1964, No. 2.

fewer obsolete preconceptions. . . . This situation is just beginning to be felt as an immediate reality in American industry, and it is this kind of uncontrollably rapid change which generates democratization.[2]

The main themes presented in this book disagree with the Bennis and Slater ideas just quoted. The view in this book is that the individual is central to the understanding of organization problems including changing concepts of management. Organizations bear the imprint of men who lead and work in them and do not evolve simply as depersonalized structures.

In his fascinating book, *The Lord of the Flies*, William Golding dealt in allegorical form with this same issue.[3] He suggested that man's nature, his psychological endowment and urges, remain as the bedrock upon which society, its organizations and institutions, must be built for good or for evil. The encounter between man who seeks to master himself and the institution in which he lives is and remains problematic. No outcome, democracy or autocracy, exists apart from the condition of man in his *lonely* quest for mastery of himself.

In Golding's novel, we are presented with a hero—a young boy—who is in intimate communication with his instinctual appetites, his fellow human beings as partial reflections of himself, and reality in the form of a crude environment. The hero's problem is to experience and master himself, his involvements with other persons, and the hostile surroundings. This battle for mastery is at once a detached and lonely struggle for the hero and an interpersonal episode since the reality requires the construction of a society suitable for the demands of survival. This reality demand is not achieved by one individual in Golding's novel, nor in actual life, so that the psychological experience for the hero and its related tensions are constantly before us.

What are the possible outcomes of this struggle and the experience of tensions? For Bennis and Slater, the outcomes are two:

[2] *Ibid.*, p. 54.
[3] William Golding, *The Lord of the Flies* (New York: Capricorn Books, 1959).

either democratization of institutions or the alternative of autocracy and authoritarianism. Democracy implies in this view subordinating the individual to a benign egalitarian organization which will take over the conflicts in mastery of self. The price of "escalating" this psychological conflict from man to the organization is individual anonymity and homogeneity. Let me quote Bennis and Slater again to enable us to experience their views more directly. The authors of "Democracy Is Inevitable" join the issue fully when they explain the need for "the organization man" as a by-product of this version of democracy in organizations:

The trend toward the "organization man" is also a trend toward a looser and more flexible organization in which the roles are to some extent interchangeable and no one is indispensable. To many people this trend is a monstrous nightmare, but one should at least not confuse it with the nightmares of the past. It may mean anonymity and homogeneity, but it does not and cannot mean authoritarianism, in the long run, despite the bizarre anomalies and hybrids that may arise in a period of transition.

The reason it cannot is that it arises out of a need for flexibility and adaptability. Democracy and the dubious trend toward the "organization man" alike (for this trend *is* a part of democratization, whether we like this aspect of democracy or not) arise from the need to maximize the availability of appropriate knowledge, skill, and insight under conditions of great variability.[4]

The organization and its requirements become, then, overriding forces in the process of homogenization of man. To be sure, the organization is presented in the metaphor of a benevolent and egalitarian culture, but it still dominates the solution of how man shall live and work in a society of interdependence based upon the division of effort.

Bennis and Slater avoid the contradiction in their own argument in assuming that it is possible for "skill and insight under conditions of great variability" to exist apart from fostering individuation and the experience of wholeness as a man. An individ-

[4] Bennis and Slater, *op. cit.*, p. 55.

ual cannot easily cultivate skills and competences without somehow experiencing himself. Once he does capture even a small
sense of selfhood, then he proceeds to take into himself the conflict and paradoxes of the hero as in *The Lord of the Flies.*

Much of contemporary thought is devoted to expounding the
myth of the death of the hero. We are accustomed to thinking
about the hero in the terms of the great man, a figure of Church-
illian stature who casts a deathless shadow over his times. The
myth of the death of the hero is based upon the idea that society
no longer needs the great man because, as in Bennis and Slater's
argument, institutions have rendered him obsolete.

The great man historically came upon the scene in times
of crisis. Like a Moses, he led his people out of bondage, but
upon arrival at the Promised Land he could not enter. Life in
the Promised Land apparently remained for the bureaucratic personality whether as leader or follower in organizations and society.

Only history seems to show that no sooner do we feel secure in
the Promised Land (or whatever we would like to call utopias)
than the bureaucratic solution seems to come unstuck. A new
crisis emerges and we wait expectantly for the reappearance of
the hero.

Interestingly enough, civilization has seemed to produce its
heroes who generate the life-death struggle (like a Hitler) and
who overcome the crisis through their leadership (like a Churchill).

More recently, the great magnetism and attraction of John F.
Kennedy seemed related to the vision of the hero. He had the
markings of the great man and his assassination seemed ironically
and bitterly to personify the myth of the death of the hero in its
present form.

Yet I would suggest that even in the current wave of bureaucratization the dream of the hero will be kept alive. The myth of
his death appears in the form of the ideal rationalization and
democratization of organizations or in the ideals of utopia. Both
ideals portray organizations and society that take over and solve
man's problem of managing aggression or other primitive urges.

The dream of the hero is kept alive for us by the humanist— through art, music, poetry, drama, and the novel. In his song and theme the humanist renews with vitality the tensions of man's existence. The individual in humanistic terms must struggle to master himself. The theme of struggle and mastery is reflected in a work of power like Michelangelo's "Moses" or the compelling ambiguity of Leonardo da Vinci's "Mona Lisa." The humanist communicates the song of the hero in ways that reach the deepest levels of experience.

One major theme in the portrayal of the hero is the encounter with one's own ambivalence. It is not only possible but in the very nature of human development for individuals to live within a matrix of conflicting feelings and ideas. The individual simultaneously loves and hates, seeks for active control and passive submission; feels the urge to create and to destroy; pushes forward to new challenges and looks backward to older and apparently more secure gratifications.

Organizations themselves can be viewed as reflections of man's ambivalent nature. At any given time in the history of an organization, its culture represents an attempted solution to the problem of ambivalence, particularly involving forces tending toward conservation and security, on the one hand, and innovation and change, on the other. The struggle may proceed in a hidden form, but nevertheless exists as a strong current reflecting the divided natures of men who lead and manage.

Managers and students of organizations delude themselves with the view that the bureaucratic solution solves the individual's problems. It may contain the ambivalent attitude by pushing it underground in favor of a temporary solution. The various solutions include the complete array of organization techniques and ideologies in current vogue like democracy, decentralization, participation, and management by committee. All of these temporary solutions favor the avoidance of the inner struggle through the acceptance of ideas like individual obsolescence and interchangeability.

The reason organizational solutions come unstuck derives from the impact of man's increasing ability to assert himself over nature. The scientific revolution has made it possible to overturn tradition and to innovate at a rate beyond normal comprehension. This impetus to change has hit industry and rendered obsolete commonsensical notions about the goals and strategies of corporate enterprises.

Corporations are dissolving the boundaries that set off one industry from another. Lines of competition have, therefore, become increasingly complex, placing the premium on ideas and talented individuals. The need for imaginative and innovative individuals transcends existing organization solutions. Organizational structures, therefore, typically give way to men of ideas who use themselves in increasingly creative ways.

The organizational solution, in other words, is designed to solve past problems and comes unstuck as a result of the impact of men and ideas. The creative individual who thrives on ideas and innovation is the contemporary hero. He is as singular in his times as the heroes of old who fought wars and created nations. But what the modern hero may have in common with the traditional hero is a sense of self, including both the courage to assert his individuality and the endurance to bear the pain of self-hood.

The hero lives by and understands the theme of individuality, transcending the limits of rationality inherent in the organization solutions. In the words of Emerson, the hero *needs* individuality because "Every true man is a cause, a country, and an age; requires infinite spaces and numbers and time fully to accomplish his design."[5]

The problem of individuality, particularly among individuals in the "career" classes of society, turns frequently on the types of standards the person uses in evaluating himself. Individuals carry within them internal sets of standards that have two distinctly different qualities. One set of standards consists of the ideals, those characteristics that describe what the individual hopes to realize or become. These ideals are imbedded in history and embodied in the distant heroes who have exemplified achievements toward which persons aspire.

[5] R. W. Emerson, "On Self Reliance" in *The Selected Writings of Ralph Waldo Emerson* (New York: Modern Library, 1940), p. 154.

The second type of internal standard is the restrictive conscience. Whereas the ideals utilize history to portray the forward-moving or progressive desires of the individual and as such are oriented to the future, the restrictions of conscience exist as the imperatives of "thou shalt not." They prohibit activity, restrict movement, and are oriented to the past.

The organizational solutions ally themselves with the restrictive conscience. The failure to observe the restrictive imperatives results in guilt, ostracism, and even overt punishment. When an individual feels depleted and functions with a low estimation of himself, or when he compulsively must justify himself in his own eyes, he may be overburdened by the restrictive standards and undermotivated by the positive ideals.

Action that moves toward the realization of the ideals, the positive standards, results in the augmentation of the individual's sense of self-worth. He feels worthy in the exercise of competences whose meaning is elaborated within a set of positive standards that he has incorporated within his mind.

Emerson in his essay "On Self-Reliance" portrayed the idea of self-worth through action consonant with the positive ideals:

> There is a time in every man's education when he arrives at the conviction that envy is ignorance; that imitation is suicide; that he must take himself for better or for worse as his portion; that though the wide universe is full of good, no kernel of nourishing corn can come to him but through his toil bestowed on that plot of ground which is given him to till.[6]

And Emerson expressed the view that the ideals of behavior exist within the individual who trusts himself:

> Henceforth, please God, forever I forego
> The yoke of men's opinions. I will be
> Light-hearted as a bird, and live with God.
> I find him in the bottom of my heart,
> I hear continually his voice therein.[7]

The latter-day hero uses to the fullest the positive ideals that

[6] *Ibid.*, p. 146.
[7] Emerson, "On Self Reliance," p. 815.

are an integral part of his personality. These ideals do not depend in the final analysis on validation from the environment but are, rather, autonomous characteristics deeply rooted in the individual's experience. The ideals are not derived initially from the memberships specific to time and place, but are instead universal concerns beyond situations and events.

The ideals of the hero may be experienced passively, as though they come upon him almost as a gift. But they are renewed and asserted in an active mode so that they may finally become impressed upon organizations and institutions. The hero more nearly changes situations, impelled as he is by ideals, than he is changed by them.

I have suggested that organizational solutions represent a kind of bargain in which the individual invests himself in an institution in return for which he will be given a respite from self-awareness and all the pain implied in the search for individuality. While this bargain may be a happy solution for some, it is untenable for the hero at least as here defined.

A central theme in the psychology of the hero as well as the sociology of organizations is the management of aggression. I take it, from Bennis and Slater's article, that the fear of aggression is central to their exchange of individuation for the homogenization they call democracy.

It is true that we are witness on all sides of our history to the primitive outbreak of aggression. The inhuman acts of war, scapegoating, and intolerance depend on aggressive energy in human personality. But in all cases of the inhuman use of aggression, individuals singly and collectively give up their sense of responsibility of personal acts and turn themselves over to a bureaucracy. When individuals assume personal responsibility for their own aggressive impulses, they are more likely to use their energy for constructive rather than destructive goals.

The recent trial of Adolf Eichmann is a good case in point. The trial established his direct involvement in concentration camp atrocities. But he felt no personal responsibility because he viewed himself as a hireling carrying out orders. But with this rationalization and attempt at self-justification, Eichmann tried to deny the existence of the hate and destructive urges within himself. He used the organization for "permission" to vent his personal hatred—yet the acts and the responsibility were unavoidably his since he *chose* to do what he did.

The act of choice, whether through conscious or unconscious mechanisms, places the individual in the forefront of organizational behavior. In the final analysis men think, feel, choose, and act. Responsibility for these unique forms of individual behavior cannot be abdicated in the name of organizations and institutions. Paradoxically, philosophies of organization that give primacy to the structure undermine individual choice and freedom whether in the name of democracy or autocracy.

Earlier we suggested that while some organization theorists and practitioners are inclined to elaborate the myth of the death of the hero, the humanist, traditionally, keeps the dream of the hero alive through artistic creations. It is now timely, perhaps long overdue, for educators and leaders in the professions to ally themselves with both the humanist and the scientist. This alliance is necessary in formulating the aims of professional education as well as in helping to construct its substance and methods.

The professional schools of business and management are engaged in serious re-evaluation of their objectives and philosophy. Business organizations and government are similarly engaged in re-evaluation of executive development programs. The question central to these appraisals is: What kind of man will be creative in the demands of leadership in the years ahead? The image of this man ranges from the institutionalist to the hero, from the person who orients himself completely within an institution to the one who builds his orientation from a sense of self.

An alliance of education, science, and humanism is ideally suited to the development of individualists. The integration implied in this alliance utilizes the developmental perspective—how individuals achieve increasing degrees of mastery through cultivating their minds and exercising competence. The aesthetic and ethical imperatives are implicit in this quest for mastery, since the individual builds out of himself and the commitment to responsibility over his choices.

Conditions in contemporary education favor this alliance. Specialists trained in various scientific or allied disciplines play an increasingly important role in the work of professional schools. Their strong intellectual interests coupled with the improved secondary and undergraduate work of students in the professional schools provide a receptive audience for the humanists. Along with these trends, leaders in the professions, including business, are demanding a new type of man from the schools— one who can use sophisticated technologies of thought but with the liberal mind capable of independent choice and decision.

This new breed of professionals influenced by the alliance of education, science, and humanism may in the long run make over organizations. And by his presence this new hero may counter the myth of individual obsolescence and keep alive the ideals of individuation.

Index

ABRAHAM ZALEZNIK is Professor of Organizational Behavior at Harvard University's Graduate School of Business Administration. He was born in Philadelphia, Pennsylvania, and received his A.B. degree from Alma College, and his M.B.A. and D.C.S. degrees from Harvard University. He is currently an Affiliate Member and a Research Fellow of the Boston Psychoanalytic Society and Institute, and is a consultant to various companies and government agencies in the United States and abroad. He is a member of the American Sociological Society and the Society for Applied Anthropology.

Professor Zaleznik is the author or coauthor of many books, including *Foreman Training in a Growing Enterprise* and *Worker Satisfaction and Development*.

Set in Linotype Janson
Composed, printed and bound by The Haddon Craftsmen, Inc.
HARPER & ROW, PUBLISHERS, INCORPORATED